The Patented Works of J. Hutton Pulitzer

KEYSTROKE AUTOMATOR

Patent Number: DES 432,539
Date of Patent: October 24, 2000

A Contradiction in Time

In 1985, leaving the comfortable world of a Fortune 500 company to pursue my own entrepreneurial dreams/venture was a mutually terrifying and electrifying proposition.

At that time, comfort for me was defined as "Corporate America". And my mega-corporation world included over twenty-five years spent in Senior Executive positions with AT&T, General Electric, Oracle and British Telecom.

But in 1985 I took that "leap of faith" and purchased a company whereby I could pursue my entrepreneurial dreams. In doing so, I inherited a young employee associated with that company who I immediately recognized had great potential. He was smart, quick to learn and searching for knowledge to become a powerful and influential force in both the business world and society (his career had just begun). He left an indelible impression on me, one that has been branded in my mind for over thirty years (as I write this prologue).

This initial venture in 1985 was my first into the mostly solo activities associated with the entrepreneurial world. In the 80's becoming an Entrepreneur was the "New-New". Most seasoned executives in Corporate America wanted to become one, and all had taken full notice of the ultimate entrepreneur – STEVE JOBS – as the dynamic entrepreneur who could build a huge company, and yet still move and be as nimble as a newly minted entrepreneur.

During this time, all seasoned executives were "*In Search of Excellence*" (by Tom Peters). Dreams were big and visionaries were leading the way; but few either had the nerve or possessed the willing to take the risk outside of the corporate world to be a true entrepreneur.

With that first acquisition of a small company came one individual, which would change my life in many ways. Funny, to even type that since I was the seasoned Fortune 500 Executive who was going to teach him the ways of the corporate world and this person was just barely out of his teens.

From the day, as the new company owner and meeting him, my soul knew he would accomplish great things. Great things, maybe not in the traditional orthodox manner that most people understand/expect, but in a manner that is unique to HIS way of achieving his goals for mankind. I trusted my natural instincts then and he has proven them right to this day.

Just as with any business, time marches on and things change and within a few years this young visionary left my tutelage to forge his own entrepreneurial path. Coming from the mega corporation's culture and now eighteen years as an

entrepreneur, I have had the opportunity to work with extremely talented individuals, but none can match the creative mind/talents of J. Hutton Pulitzer.

Pulitzer is the ultimate contradiction if they're ever was one. The duality of what he was and could be is amazing. On one hand an incredible presenter and salesman, while on the other a loner/society recluse. An incredible technical genius that does not write a lick of code, a maniacal visionary who often runs and thinks too fast for the average person, but yet continually alters his activities to help others to understand and/or succeed; but yet probably cares too much about what people think at times.

Truly a contradiction:

Like Steve Jobs, Pulitzer's mind thinks and works differently when it comes to life and impacting society in multiple ways. One of his most cherished achievements was the development and implementation of the world's first "global positioning system for the Internet" (i.e. the CueCat™). Definitely ahead of the times, Pulitzer's vision for accessing the Internet in a unique manner was sponsored and financed by such corporate giants as RadioShack, ING Barings, Coca-Cola, NBC, etc. for a total of $200 million and successful individuals such as Steven Spielberg, Steve Forbes, etc. Top manufacturers and corporations throughout the world understood and invested in the :CRQ Cue Code technology because they shared Pulitzer's vision and knew it would "bridge the gap" between consumers and their companies. But consumers were slow to "understand" the new technology and the Internet market crash in 2000-2001 ended the rapid success of his company's (Digital Convergence, Inc.) technology in its initial form; but yet still today, over two billion consumers around the world a day utilize some derivative of his initial patents.

Nevertheless, Pulitzer's patents and his creative visions continue to thrive in today's highly complex and technological environment. Even today, when you board an American Airlines flight, the boarding agent utilizes a derivative of Pulitzer's scanning patent when he/she scans your Boarding Pass for the flight. And Smart Phones of all types/manufacturers utilize the patented technology that Pulitzer originally invented with his Chief Technology Officer at Digital Convergence in the late 1990's.

Bottom line, society should not dismiss or misjudge Pulitzer in the future. Other entrepreneurs like him who themselves have failed several times in their careers have proven to be geniuses when their total careers are evaluated. Pulitzer is the ultimate Type "A" personality and he continues to think creatively and decisively, which in time will certainly impact our lives again...... I can guarantee this!

To this day, more than 30 years later, we still work together. It is certainly a challenge to work beside him but I feel honored to be his co-worker and friend. Today our roles have changed and I am learning from him. To understand him is

to learn to love him and his personification of a contradiction. Fact is he does not let many inside personally; whether its too painful or he is just too driven and focused, remains to be seen. But you have to respect his accomplishments and recognize that there is more than one way to accomplish greatness.

That's my personal dialog about Hutton, but if I were talking to a business executive who was inquiring about Hutton and wanting to know "if the myths about him are true" I would answer in the following manner:

As a trusted and extraordinary individual, J. Hutton Pulitzer has continually demonstrated a unique ability to see ahead in time and forecast the future with an uncanny degree of accuracy. Many times over the past 32 years that I have known him, he has creatively and successfully leveraged his visions of the future in order to insure the success of many types of business ventures.

Having experienced the agony of competitive inroads associated with some of his early projects, Hutton quickly studied all aspects surrounding the sophisticated art of drafting patents and has "mastered" the ability to author and construct patents in a manner that are "iron clad" in blocking competitive inroads by outside entities. His effectiveness can be substantiated via his present patent portfolio, which includes global patents granted in 189 countries (a feat most inventors never attain).

His unique and personal approach in constructing patents has proven to be extremely successful which is further substantiated by his single best unmatched patent ratio of forty-nine citations per one patent (i.e. 49:1 ratio) and the fact that he currently holds an unparalleled patent granted record of 98.8%.

In addition to authoring unique and complex patents, he is extremely experienced in the art of constructing original patents in such a manner as to anticipate future potential infringements associated with any/all patents he writes. Hutton takes a multi-dimensional view of possible competitive inroads, as well as, the anticipation of the creative and unique ways in which his patents can be implemented. Thereby, re-enforcing the protection armor in which he builds into each and every patent he develops.

Bottom-line, his patent expertise routinely exceeds his client's and/or the industry's expectations; while effectively insuring each and every patent he develops in such a manner as to prevent any potential work around and/or patent penetration in future years. As a result, patent experts from around the world routinely keep a keen eye on Mr. Pulitzer's patent work and filings in order to possibly anticipate his vision and actions regarding the future.

As the result of Pulitzer's developing an industry around connecting codes where one did not exist before, he became the "Father" of what is now known as "Scan-To-Connect" and "Scan Commerce". Two brand new features Hutton bestowed upon the Internet in the late 90's.

But with every new industry and technology comes competition and jealously; therefore I will quote one Billionaire's comment about Pulitzer's idea for bar codes to connect to the Internet via scanning:

"The stupidest invention ever!"

That quote, which was carried by numerous newspapers, magazines and blogs when uttered was like the shot heard around the world at the time the dot com industry was crashing in 2000-2001.

But like Steve Jobs, Pulitzer is a patient man and visionaries do NOT let their dreams die. Pulitzer implemented his vision and pursued his patents for "Scan to Commerce" and "Scan to Connect" and as I mentioned above, today over two billion people around the world utilize a derivative of his original scanning patents on a daily basis. ***A multibillion-dollar industry created from the vision of a "contradiction in time".***

I say, in closing *"Two Billion daily users of his technology a day! Not bad for the stupidest invention ever*!"

Can't wait to see his next stupid idea!

Blaine L. Thacker, Ex-Corporate Executive & Entrepreneur

P.S. You should view the movie "JOBS" (i.e. Steve Jobs) to truly understand and appreciate J. Hutton Pulitzer.

US00D432539S

United States Patent [19]

Philyaw

[11] **Patent Number:** **Des. 432,539**

[45] **Date of Patent:** ** **Oct. 24, 2000**

[54] **KEYSTROKE AUTOMATOR**

[75] Inventor: **Jeffry Jovan Philyaw**, Dallas, Tex.

[73] Assignee: **DigitalConvergence.:Com Inc.**, Dallas, Tex.

[**] Term: **14 Years**

[21] Appl. No.: **29/116,705**

[22] Filed: **Jan. 7, 2000**

[51] **LOC (7) Cl.** **14-02**
[52] **U.S. Cl.** **D14/426**; D14/420
[58] **Field of Search** .... D14/420, 426, D14/427, 432, 402, 403, 405, 407, 409, 417; 235/472.01, 472.02, 472.03, 375; 345/156–167; 200/5 R, 5 A, 6 R, 6 A; 273/148 B; 74/471 XY; 463/36, 37, 38

[56] **References Cited**

U.S. PATENT DOCUMENTS

D. 343,829	2/1994	Okuda et al.	D14/426
D. 352,939	11/1994	Karlin	D14/426
D. 375,748	11/1996	Hartman	D14/417
D. 381,661	7/1997	Althans	D14/417
D. 385,263	10/1997	Taylor	D14/407

Primary Examiner—Kay H. Chin
Attorney, Agent, or Firm—Howison, Chauza, Handley & Arnott, LLP

[57] **CLAIM**

The ornamental design for keystroke automator, as shown and described.

DESCRIPTION

FIG. **1** is top view of a keystroke automator showing my new design;
FIG. **2** is right side view of the keystroke automator;
FIG. **3** is bottom view of the keystroke automator;
FIG. **4** is a left side view of the keystroke automator;
FIG. **5** is a front view of the keystroke automator; and,
FIG. **6** is rear view of the keystroke automator.
The broken lines shown in FIGS. **1** through **6** drawing are for illustrative purposes only and form no part of the claimed design.

1 Claim, 2 Drawing Sheets

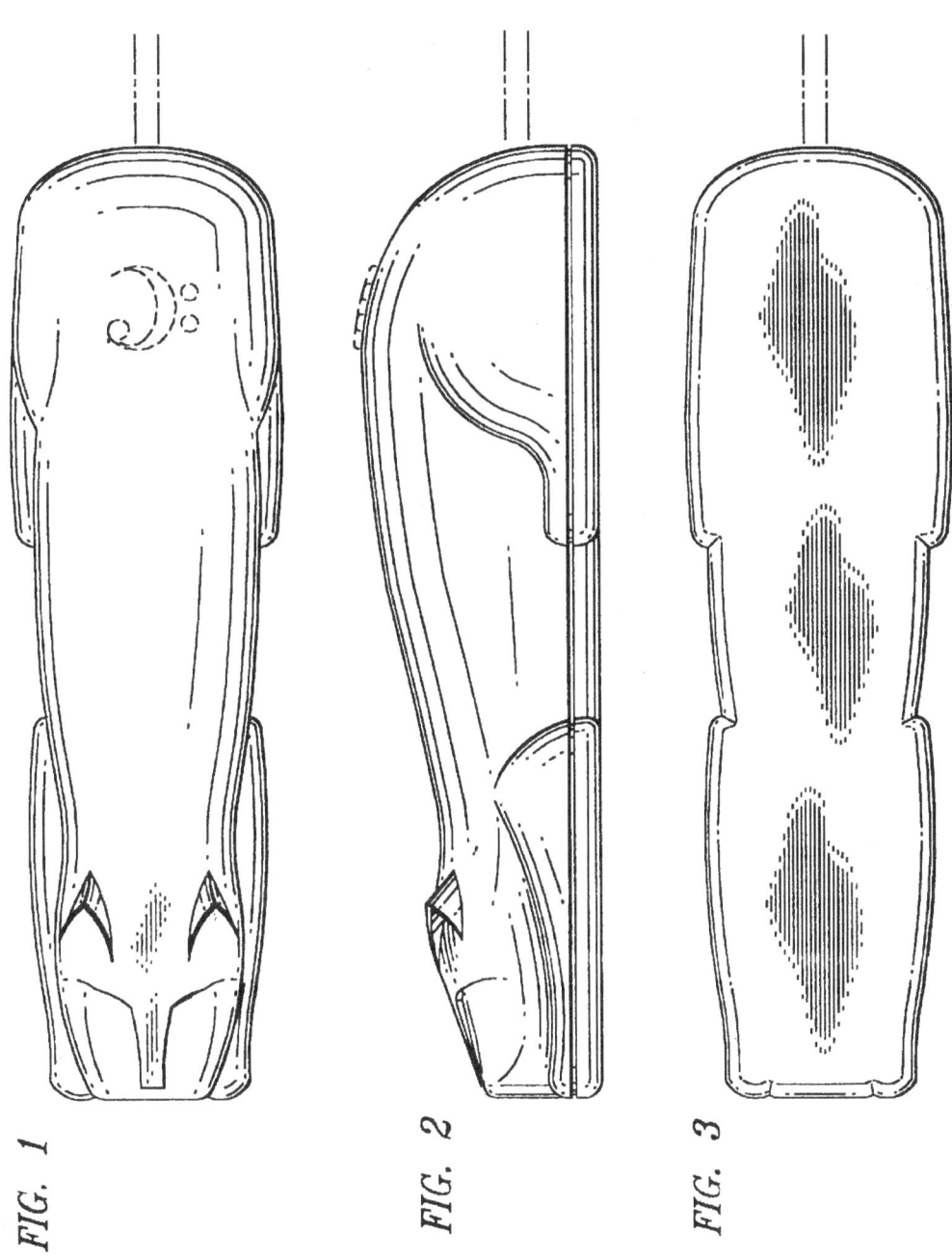

FIG. 1

FIG. 2

FIG. 3

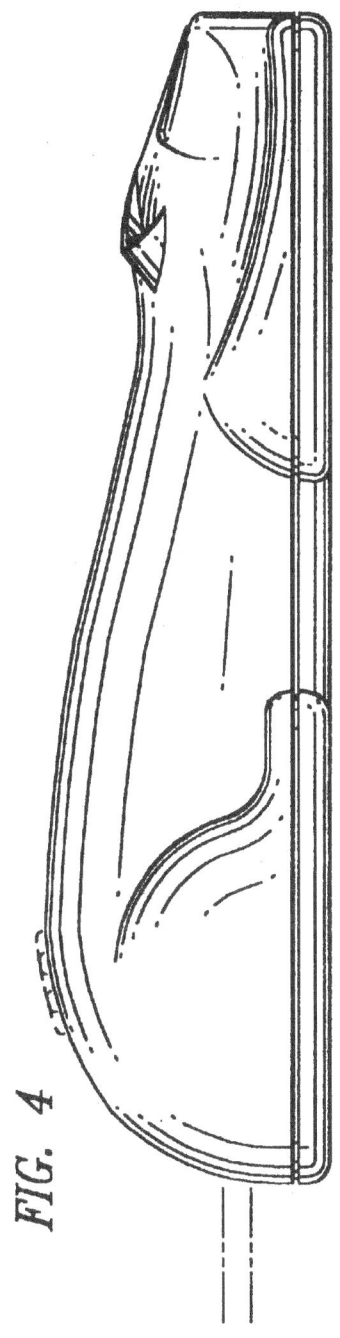

FIG. 4

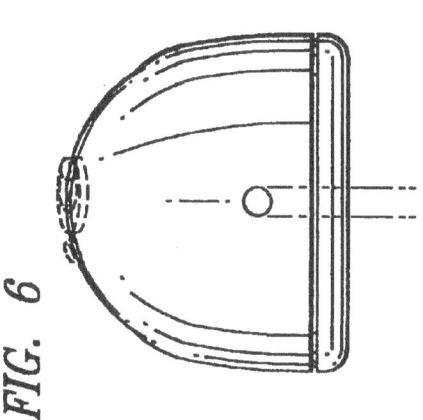

FIG. 6

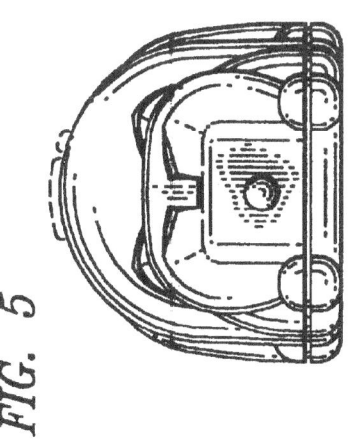

FIG. 5

Launching a web site using a passive transponder

United States 8,028,036

Issued September 27, 2011

A method of displaying a web page to a user. A triggering device (2502) having a unique code stored therein is provided to the user. The unique code is extracted from the triggering device (2502) with an activation system (302), the activation system (302) disposed on a network (306). Location information associated with the unique code is retrieved from a database (1614 or 310), the location...

Method and apparatus for utilizing an audibly coded signal to conduct commerce over the internet

United States 8,005,985

Issued August 23, 2011

A method and apparatus for utilizing a coded audio/video signal to conduct commerce over the Internet. Broadcast information is broadcast from a remote location on a secondary network containing video over the secondary network to a location thereon proximate the location of the user PC. Unique information is encoded in the broadcast information representative of a location on the primary network...

Software downloading using a television broadcast channel

United States 7,996,552

Issued August 9, 2011

 A software distribution architecture having a television broadcast system as its infrastructure. Software from a software repository (1600) is mixed into a television broadcast system and transmitted into one or more selected channels at prescribed dates and times. An at-home subscriber, capable of receiving with a receiver (1608) the one or more select channels, switches to the one or more...

Method and apparatus for connecting a user location to one of a plurality of destination locations on a network

United States 7,979,576

Issued July 12, 2011

A method for interconnecting a user's location to a destination location on a network. The unique information is received at the user's location, which unique information has no associated routing information embedded therein. Network routing information is associated with the received unique information in response to receipt thereof. The user's location is then interconnected to the...

Launching a web site using a passive transponder

United States 7,975,022

Issued July 5, 2011

A method of displaying a web page to a user. A triggering device having a unique code stored therein is provided to the user. The unique code is extracted from the triggering device with an activation system, the activation system disposed on a network. Location information associated with the unique code is retrieved from a database, the location information corresponding to a location of the...

Method and apparatus for completing, securing and conducting an E-commerce transaction

United States 7,930,213

Issued

A method of conducting and on-line transaction. A user at a PC (302) of a first location completes a profile information sheet and transmits it across a secure network (2708) to a central registration server (2704) at a second location also disposed on the network (306). The central registration server (2704) transmits a unique bar code and associated unique ID back to the user PC (302) at the...

Method for connecting a wireless device to a remote location on a network

United States 7,925,780

Issued April 12, 2011

A method for connecting a wireless device to a remote location on a computer network. A beacon signal is transmitted from a beacon unit to a beacon signal receiver circuit disposed with a wireless device. The beacon signal includes components indicative of a first code associated with a remote location and of a second code associated with an attribute of the beacon unit. A first message packet...

Input device for allowing input of unique digital code to a user's computer to control access thereof to a web site

United States 7,912,961

Issued March 22, 2011

A method for controlling a computer is disclosed wherein one or more remote locations disposed on a network are accessed in response to scanning an optical code. A first computer disposed on the network connects to a scanner for scanning the optical code of a product by a user. The scanner is uniquely identified with a scanner distributor by a scanner identification number. A second computer...

Method and apparatus for utilizing a unique transaction code to update a magazine subscription over the internet

United States 7,912,760

Issued March 22, 2011

A method for completing an electronic commerce transaction over a global communication network initiated between a vendor and a potential consumer. The method includes the steps of associating a unique transaction code with the initiated transaction between the vendor and the potential consumer for use by the consumer in completing a specific electronic commerce transaction; associating user...

Automatic configuration of equipment software

United States 7,908,467

Issued

An architecture for automatically configuring software of a piece of equipment. The piece of equipment is in communication with a network, the piece of equipment having one or more machine-resolvable codes associated therewith. The piece of equipment connects to a remote location disposed on the network in response to reading a select one of the one or more machine-resolvable codes with a reader....

Accessing a vendor web site using personal account information retrieved from a credit card company web site

United States 7,904,344

Issued March 8, 2011

A method of accessing a vendor web site (3422) over a global communication packet-switched network (306) using personal account information of a credit card (3400) retrieved from a credit card company server (3300) on the network (306). At a user location disposed on the network, a machine-resolvable code (MRC) (3402) of the credit card (3400) of a user is read with a reading device (3410). Coded...

Method and apparatus for utilizing an audible signal to induce a user to select an E-commerce function

United States 7,900,224

Issued March 1, 2011

A method for delivering advertising to a consumer over a broadcast media/global communication network combination. An advertisement broadcast is generated comprised of a general program and associated advertising dispersed there through for broadcast over a broadcast media which is directed to a general class of consumers. Unique information is embedded in the broadcast for inducing a consumer to...

Method and apparatus for accessing a remote location by receiving a product code

United States 7,886,017

Issued February 8, 2011

A method for controlling a computer is disclosed wherein one or more remote locations disposed on a network are accessed in response to accessing a product code. A first computer

disposed on the network connects to a device for accessing the product code of a product by a user. The device is uniquely identified with a device distributor by a device identification number. A second computer...

Input device having positional and scanning capabilities

United States 7,870,189

Issued January 11, 2011

A multi-purpose input device (2500) for providing conventional positional tracking, and one or more read capabilities for automatically connecting a user PC (302) to remote node. In one embodiment, a user reads optically encoded indicia (1606) of a product by passing the input device (2500) thereover. A software interface (2505) processes the read information, assembles a message packet, and...

Method for interfacing scanned product information with a source for the product over a global network

United States 7,822,829

Issued October 26, 2010

A method for interfacing scanned product information with a source for the product over a global network. A method is provided for obtaining information regarding the source of a product from a remote information source location on a global communication network utilizing a product code associated with the product and unique thereto. The product code associated with the product is scanned with a...

Portable scanner for enabling automatic commerce transactions

United States 7,819,316

Issued October 26, 2010

A method for initiating and completing a commercial transaction is disclosed that allows a user to acquire and own an article of commerce having associated therewith a machine resolvable code (MRC), the MRC having encoded therein information relating to the article of commerce, the user having unique identification information associated with the user. The MRC is first recognized and a...

Retrieving personal account information from a web site by reading a credit card

United States 7,818,423

Issued October 19, 2010

A method of accessing personal account information of a credit card (3400) over a global communication packet-switched network (306). At a user location disposed on the network (306), a machine-resolvable code (MRC) (3402) of the credit card (3400) of a user is read with a reading device (3410). Coded information is extracted from the MRC (3402). Routing information associated with the coded...

Method and apparatus for allowing a broadcast to remotely control a computer

United States 7,792,696

Issued September 6, 2010

The present invention disclosed and claimed herein comprises a system and method for launching an advertisement on a computer having an audio input interface and a display; an audio output acoustically coupled from a broadcast source to the input interface for outputting an audio signal having encoded therein an advertisement; and a program operable on the computer and responsive to the audio...

Launching a web site using a personal device

United States Launching a web site using a personal device

Issued June 15, 2010

A method of displaying a web page to a user. A triggering device (2500) is provided having a unique code associated therewith, the unique code associated with a remote location on a network of the source of the web page. The unique code is transmitted from the triggering device (2500) to an interface system (302), which interface system (302) is disposed on the network (306) at a triggering...

Network routing utilizing a product code

United States 7,694,020

Issued April 6, 2010

A method for utilizing a product code having product information contained therein for interfacing over a network. A representation of the product information is extracted from the product code, which product code is disposed on or in close association with an associated product. In response to this extraction, network routing information is associated with the product code information.

Method and apparatus for automatic configuration of equipment

United States 7,653,446

Issued January 26, 2010

An architecture for automatically configuring equipment. A piece of equipment connected externally to a user PC has one or more machine-resolvable codes (MRCs) associated therewith. The piece of equipment receives configuration information from a remote location disposed on the network in response to reading a select one of the one or more MRCs with a reader. Configuration information associated...

Method and apparatus for matching a user's use profile in commerce with a broadcast

United States 7,636,788

Issued

A method for advertising over a network and broadcast media combination. A user's computer at a location on the network is operable to receive a signal from a broadcast generated by an advertiser, which signal has embedded therein unique coded information. The user's computer is connected to an advertiser's location in response to extracting a representation of the audio signal...

Method and apparatus for utilizing an existing product code to issue a match to a predetermined location on a global network

United States 7,596,786

Issued September 29, 2009

A method for providing an interconnection relationship between a product and a desired location on a global communications network. A machine readable product code is disposed on the product machine readable product code, the machine readable product code having encoded product information contained therein. The product code has no routing information embedded therein which would allow the...

Method for configuring a piece of equipment with the use of an associated machine resolvable code

United States 7,558,838

Issued July 7, 2009

An architecture for automatically configuring equipment interfaced to a computer. A computer which is in communication with a network, is provided having the piece of equipment interfaced to the computer and having associated therewith one or more machine-resolvable codes (MRCs). The computer connects to a remote location disposed on the network in response to a select one of the one or more MRCs...

Software downloading using a television broadcast channel

United States 7,548,988

Issued June 16, 2009

A software distribution architecture having a television broadcast system as its infrastructure. Software from a software repository (1600) is mixed into a television broadcast system and transmitted into one or more selected channels at prescribed dates and times. An at-home subscriber, capable of receiving with a receiver (1608) the one or more select channels, switches to the one or more...

Method and apparatus for opening and launching a web browser in response to an audible signal

United States 7,536,478

Issued May 19, 2009

The present invention disclosed and claimed herein comprises a system and method for launching a web browser on a network comprising a computer having an all new input interface and a communication interface coupled to a computer network; said audio input coupled to the audio output of a source for receiving an audio signal having encoded therein a unique code that is associated with a...

Method and apparatus for accessing a remote location with an optical reader having a programmable memory system

United States 7,533,177

Issued May 12, 2009

A method of accessing a remote location on a network using an optical reader. The optical reader includes an optical scanning system, a programmable memory system and an output circuit and is user-switchable between a scan mode, a record mode and a playback mode. The optical reader transmits a code to a first computer disposed on the network. When the optical reader is in the scan mode, the code...

Method for interconnecting two locations over a network in response to using a tool

United States 7,526,532

Issued April 28, 2009

A method for accessing information over a network. A tool is utilized in conjunction with an operation on a user's processor at a user location on the network. The tool has associated therewith a unique tool ID. In response to utilizing the tool, the user's location is interconnected on the network to a predetermined destination at a remote location on the network, which destination has...

Control of software interface with information input to access window

United States 7,523,161

Issued April 21, 2009

A method is disclosed for controlling the software interface of a user's computing device to display information on a display in proximity to the physical location of the user's computing device. The interface is operable to display to a user on the display at least one access window that is operable to access information about a product, which access window requires the user to input a...

Method and apparatus for utilizing a unique transaction code to update a magazine subscription over the internet

United States 7,505,922

Issued March 17, 2009

The present invention disclosed herein comprises a method for completing an electronic commerce transaction over a global communication network initiated between a vendor and a

potential consumer. The method includes the steps of associating a unique transaction code with the initiated transaction between the vendor and the potential consumer for use by the consumer in completing a specific...

Launching a web site using a portable scanner

United States 7,496,638

Issued February 24, 2009

A method for a user to access information on a network. Information from a machine recognizable code (MRC) (1606) is extracted at a user location, which MRC (1606) has associated therewith routing information to a remote location (312) on the network. The extracted information from the MRC (1606) is wirelessly transmitted to a network interface device (302) in response to the information being...

Controlling a PC using a tone from a cellular telephone

United States 7,493,384

Issued February 17, 2009

A method and apparatus for accessing information over a network (306) from a remote location (312) on the network (306) for delivery to a user PC (302). A cellular telephone (2500) is provided having a functional mode for web access over the network (306). A button (2502) on the phone is associated with the functional mode. The button on the phone (2500) is activated by a user to induce the...

Performing an e-commerce transaction from credit card account information retrieved from a credit card company web site

United States 7,493,283

Issued February 17, 2009

A method of conducting an e-commerce transaction on a global communication network (306) by using personal account information of a credit card retrieved from a credit card company server on the network (306). At a user location disposed on the network, a machine-resolvable code (MRC) (3402) of the credit card (3400) of a user is read with a reading device (3410). Coded information is extracted...

Method and apparatus for allowing a remote site to interact with an intermediate database to facilitate access to the remote site

United States 7,487,259

Issued February 3, 2009

Method and apparatus for allowing a remote site to interact with an intermediate database to facilitate access to the remote site a method for delivering information from a source on a global communication network to destination location thereon. A unique code is associated with an advertising action associated with the source location. The unique code is stored in a database and routing...

Method and apparatus for launching a web browser in response to scanning of product information

United States 7,440,993

Issued October 21, 2008

A method for interconnecting a user's location to a destination location on a network. The unique information is received at the user's location, which unique information has no associated routing information embedded therein. Network routing information is associated with the received unique information in response to receipt thereof. The user's location is then interconnected to the...

Method and apparatus for utilizing an audibly coded signal to conduct commerce over the internet

United States 7,437,475

Issued October 14, 2008

A Method and apparatus for utilizing a coded audio/video signal to conduct commerce over the Internet. Broadcast information is broadcast from a remote location on a secondary network containing video over the secondary network to a location thereon proximate the location of the user PC. Unique information is encoded in the broadcast information representative of a location on the primary network...

Input device for allowing interface to a web site in association with a unique input code

United States 7,428,499

Issued September 23, 2008

An input device for allowing interface to a web site in association with a unique input code. A method for interconnecting a first location on a global communication network with a second location thereon is disclosed. An input device is provided at the first location on the global communication network having associated therewith a unique input device ID. A product code disposed on a product is...

Method using database for facilitating computer based access to a location on a network after scanning a barcode disposed on a product

United States 7,424,521

Issued September 9, 2008

A visual indicia for facilitating computer based access of a network by consumer. A machine readable code is disposed on a surface having encoded therein information as to a product or a surface, which machine readable code has no routing information contained therein to allow a user to access any location on a network. A visual indicia is disposed on the surface indicative of a relationship...

Method for interfacing scanned product information with a source for the product over a global network

United States 7,415,511

Issued August 19, 2008

A method for interfacing scanned product information with a source for the product over a global network. A method is provided for obtaining information regarding the source of a product from a remote information source location on a global communication network utilizing a product code associated with the product and unique thereto. The product code associated with the product is scanned with a...

Method for conducting a contest using a network

United States 7,412,666

Issued August 12, 2008

A method for conducting a contest using a network is provided. A plurality of pick spaces, a virtual display fixture, and a plurality of virtual articles of commerce are displayed on the screen of a user computer. The user computer is disposed at a user site and operably connected to the network. Initially, the virtual articles of commerce are arrayed on the virtual display fixture. At least one...

Method and apparatus for controlling a user's pc through a broadcast communication to archive information in the user's pc

United States 7,398,548

Issued July 8, 2008

A method for allowing a consumer to access an advertiser's location over a global communication network. A normal broadcast program is broadcast to a class of consumers having a unique signal embedded therein, which unique signal embedded therein is associated with a particular advertiser and a predetermined location on the network. Additionally, the unique signal has encoded therein a unique...

Portable scanner for enabling automatic commerce transactions

United States 7,392,945

Issued July 1, 2008

A method for initiating and completing a commercial transaction to acquire an article of commerce (2502). The article of commerce (2502) has associated therewith a machine resolvable code (MRC) (2504). The MRC (2504) has encoded therein information relating to the article of commerce (2502). The encoded information in the MRC (2504) is extracted therefrom and unique identification information...

Method for utilizing visual cue in conjunction with web access

United States 7,392,312

Issued June 24, 2008

The use of a visual indicia or cue facilitates computer based access of a network by a consumer witnessing a presentation. A visual indicia or cue is provided during the presentation indicative of a relationship between the visual indicia or cue in the presence of a location on a network. This allows this location on the network to be accessed by a computer having an appropriate input device for...

Method for conducting a contest using a network

United States 7,392,285

Issued June 24, 2008

A method for conducting a contest using a network is provided. A plurality of pick spaces and a rolling counter are displayed on a screen of a computer operably connected to the network at a user site. The rolling counter constitutes successive ones of a plurality of available characters, each character being displayed for a preselected duration. Each time the user performs a predefined selection...

Launching a web site using a personal device

United States 7,386,600

Issued June 10, 2008

A method of displaying a web page to a user. A triggering device (2500) is provided having a unique code associated therewith, the unique code associated with a remote location on a network of the source of the web page. The unique code is transmitted from the triggering device (2500) to an interface system (302), which interface system (302) is disposed on the network (306) at a triggering...

Method and apparatus for tracking user profile and habits on a global network

United States 7,383,333

Issued June 3, 2008

A method and apparatus for tracking network activity of a user. A user PC (302) disposed on a network (306) runs tracking software which initially requires registration to a registration server (2500). The registration process is initiated by the user entering user information into the tracking software for transmission to the registration server (2500). In response to registration, the...

Method and apparatus for accessing a remote location with a reader having a dedicated memory system

United States 7,383,319

Issued June 3, 2008

A method of accessing a remote location on a network using an optical reader. The optical reader has an optical scanning system and a dedicated address memory system. The optical scanning system, in response to the user scanning an encoded indicia therewith, sends to a first computer disposed on the network a scan code indicative of information encoded in the scanned indicia. The dedicated...

Accessing a vendor web site using personal account information retrieved from a credit card company web site

United States 7,379,901

Issued May 27, 2008

A method of accessing a vendor web site (3422) over a global communication packet-switched network (306) using personal account information of a credit card (3400) retrieved from a credit card company server (3300) on the network (306). At a user location disposed on the network, a machine-resolvable code (MRC) (3402) of the credit card (3400) of a user is read with a reading device (3410). Coded...

Software downloading using a television broadcast channel

United States 7,370,114

Issued May 6, 2008

A software distribution architecture having a television broadcast system as its infrastructure. Software from a software repository (1600) is mixed into a television broadcast system and transmitted into one or more selected channels at prescribed dates and times. An at-home subscriber, capable of receiving with a receiver (1608) the one or more select channels, switches to the one or more...

Presentation of web page content based upon computer video resolution

United States 7,346,694

Issued March 18, 2008

An architecture for customizing the amount of web page banner advertising content presented to a user. When a user accesses a server node (102) disposed on a network (104), the user computer (100) provides video resolution information to the server node (102). The server node (102) transmits a web page to the user node (100) which corresponds to the video resolution information of the user node...

Network routing utilizing a product code

United States 7,321,941

Issued January 22, 2008

A method for utilizing a product code having product information contained therein for interfacing over a network. The product information is extracted from the product code, which product code is disposed on or in close association with an associated product. In response to this extraction, network routing information is associated with the product code information

Method and apparatus for utilizing an audibly coded signal to conduct commerce over the internet

United States 7,318,106

Issued January 8, 2008

A Method and apparatus for utilizing an audibly coded signal to conduct commerce over the Internet. Broadcast information is broadcast from a remote location on a secondary network over the secondary network to a location, thereon proximate the location of the user PC on a primary network. Unique information is encoded in the broadcast information representative of a location on the primary...

Optical reader with ultraviolet wavelength capability

United States 7,314,173

Issued January 1, 2008

An optical reader is provided for reading a bar code having ultraviolet-wavelength-responsive properties. The optical reader includes an ultraviolet light source, a photodetector, an optical system and a decoder. The ultraviolet light source generates ultraviolet light having a wavelength shorter than visible light and longer than X-rays for illuminating a target region. The photodetector...

Method and apparatus for automatic configuration of equipment

United States 7,308,483

Issued December 11, 2007

An architecture for automatically configuring equipment. A piece of equipment connected externally to a user PC has one or more machine-resolvable codes (MRCs) associated therewith. The piece of equipment receives configuration information from a remote location disposed on the network in response to reading a select one of the one or more MRCs with a reader. Configuration information associated...

Aiming indicia for a bar code and method of use

United States 7,296,746

Issued

An aiming indicia is provided for a bar code comprising a sequence of parallel code bars and intervening code spaces disposed along a longitudinal code axis in accordance with a predefined standard. The aiming indicia comprises a non-encoded graphic element disposed on the longitudinal code axis adjacent the bar code and spaced apart from the nearest code bars by a distance of at least 10 times a...

Method and apparatus for opening and launching a web browser in response to an audible signal

United States 7,287,091

Issued October 23, 2007

The present invention disclosed and claimed herein comprises a system and method for launching a web browser on a network comprising a computer having an all new input interface and a communication interface coupled to a computer network; said audio input coupled to the audio output of a source for receiving an audio signal having encoded therein a unique code that is associated with a...

Method and apparatus for matching a user's use profile in commerce with a broadcast

United States 7,284,066

Issued October 16, 2007

A method for advertising over a network and broadcast media combination. A user's computer at a location on the network is operable to receive a signal from a broadcast generated by an advertiser, which signal has embedded therein unique coded information. The user's computer

is connected to an advertiser's location in response to extracting the unique coded information from the audio...

Bar code scanner and software interface interlock for performing encrypted handshaking and for disabling the scanner or input device in case of handshaking operation failure

United States 7,257,619

Issued August 14, 2007

An interlocking architecture for a software interface and a bar code scanner. Upon power-up, a handshaking operation is performed between a scanner (1600) having a scanner processor (2600) and a computer processor (2612) of a computer (302) based upon the code stored in the NV memory (2602) of the scanner (1600) and a unique code associated with the software interface running on the computer...

Digital ID for selecting web browser and use preferences of a user during use of a web application

United States 7,257,614

Issued August 14, 2007

A browser configuration architecture where input of a unique user ID automatically configures those browser applications preselected for auto-configuration from entries of a user preferences sheet. The user preferences sheet (2500) is part of the browser control software (2502) used for storing user preferences associated with one or more browser applications (2506, 2508, and 2510) loaded on a...

Optical reader and use

United States 7,240,840

Issued July 10, 2007

An optical reader is provided for reading a symbol representing information having areas of different light reflectivity. The optical reader comprises a radiant energy source, a photodetector, an optical system and a decoder. The radiant energy source generates a radiant energy for illuminating a target region. The photodetector generates output electrical signals indicative of the radiant energy...

Automatic configuration of equipment software

United States 7,237,104

Issued June 26, 2007

An architecture for automatically configuring software of a piece of equipment. The piece of equipment is in communication with a network, the piece of equipment having one or more machine-resolvable codes associated therewith. The piece of equipment connects to a remote location disposed on the network in response to reading a select one of the one or more machine-resolvable codes with a reader....

Method and apparatus for directing an existing product code to a remote location

United States 7,228,282

Issued June 5, 2007

A method for interfacing a user location on a network to a destination location on the network is disclosed. A bar code having product information contained therein relating to an associated product is first scanned with a scanner, which bar code has no network routing information contained therein. The product information contained within the bar code is then extracted. Routing information over...

Method and apparatus for accessing a remote location with an optical reader having a dedicated memory system

United States 7,197,543

Issued March 27, 2007

A method of accessing a remote location on a network using an optical reader. The optical reader has an optical scanning system and a dedicated address memory system. The optical scanning system, in response to the user scanning an encoded indicia therewith, sends to a first computer disposed on the network a scan code indicative of information encoded in the scanned indicia. The dedicated...

Method for connecting a wireless device to a remote location on a network

United States 7,191,247

Issued March 13, 2007

A method for connecting a wireless device to a remote location on a computer network. A beacon signal is transmitted from a beacon unit disposed at a first geographic location. The beacon signal includes components indicative of a first code and of a second code, the first code being associated with a remote location on a computer network and the second code being associated with an attribute of...

Method and apparatus for utilizing an existing product code to issue a match to a predetermined location on a global network

United States 7,159,037

Issued January 2, 2007

A method for providing an interconnection relationship between a product and a desired location on a global communications network. A machine readable product code is disposed on the product machine readable product code, the machine readable product code having encoded product information contained therein. The product code has no routing information embedded therein which would allow the...

Method and apparatus for launching a web site with non-standard control input device

United States 7,117,240

Issued October 3, 2006

A method for launching a web browser application on a user's computer. A browser application is provided on the user's computer that is launchable in response to predetermined browser inputs being received by the user's computer. A non-browser input is provided that is not a

portion of the set of predetermined browser inputs. This non-browser is correlated to the input to simulate one...

Battery pack having integral optical reader for wireless communication device

United States 7,089,291

Issued August 8, 2006

A battery pack for a wireless communication device comprises a housing, at least one battery disposed within the housing and an optical reader disposed within the housing. The housing is adapted to be removably attachable to a wireless communication device. The housing includes an external shell defining an optical port there through and has an operational power interface and a data interface...

Method and apparatus for controlling a user's PC through an audio-visual broadcast to archive information in the user's PC

United States 7,069,582

Issued June 27, 2006

A method for allowing a consumer to access an advertiser's location over a global communication network. A normal broadcast program is broadcast to a class of consumers having a unique signal embedded therein, which unique signal embedded therein is associated with a particular advertiser and a predetermined location on the network. Additionally, the unique signal has encoded therein a unique...

Method for controlling a computer using an embedded unique code in the content of CD media

United States 7,043,536

Issued April 9, 2006

A method for allowing a user PC (1702) to be controlled in order to effect a connection between the user PC (1702) and a destination node (1706) on a network (306). This is facilitated through an audio source (1700) wherein compact disk recording media has embedded therein an audio signal. When the compact disk recording media is played, the audio signal is extracted by an audio extractor (1600)...

Method of controlling a computer using an embedded unique code in the content of DVD media

United States 7,010,577

Issued March 7, 2006

A method for allowing a user PC to be controlled in order to effect a connection between the user PC and a destination node on a network. This is facilitated through an audio source wherein the content of digital video disk recording media has embedded therein an audio signal. When the recording media is played, the audio signal is extracted by an audio extractor and transmitted to the user PC,...

Method and apparatus for allowing a remote site to interact with an intermediate database to facilitate access to the remote site

United States 6,985,962

Issued January 10, 2006

Method and apparatus for allowing a remote site to interact with an intermediate database to facilitate access to the remote site a method for delivering information from a source on a global communication network to a second and a user location thereon. A unique code is associated with an advertising action associated with the source location. The unique code is stored in a database and routing...

Input device for allowing input of a unique digital code to a user's computer to control access thereof to a web site

United States 6,985,954

Issued January 10, 2006

An input device for allowing input of a unique digital code to a user's computer to control access thereof to a web site. A method for connecting a user computer at a first location on a network with a second location on the network through use of a coded symbol having contained therein encoded information associated with routing information on the network to the second location thereover is...

Audible designation for a node on a communication network

United States 6,981,059

Issued December 27, 2005

An audible designation for a node on a communication network A method is provided for allowing any of a plurality of first locations on a global communication network to access a specific and determinable second location on the global communication network. A unique audio signature is defined for the specific and determinable second location on the global communication network, which unique audio...

Method and apparatus for delivering information from a remote site on a network based on statistical information

United States 6,973,438

Issued December 6, 2006

A method and apparatus are disclosed for delivering information, from a content location on a global communication network (GCN) dynamically selected according to statistical information, to a user location thereon. In a computer database, GCN routing information for each of a plurality of content locations on the GCN are associated with a predefined combination of one of a plurality of...

Method for conducting a contest using a network

United States 6,970,916

Issued November 29, 2005

A method for conducting a contest using a network is provided. Displayed, on a practical screen of a user computer operably connected to the network at a user site, is a plurality of pick spaces, a virtual television set including a first virtual screen, and a virtual computer including a second virtual screen. The apparent area of the first virtual screen constitutes a first display area of the...

Method and apparatus for embedding routing information to a remote web site in an audio/video track

United States 6,970,914

Issued November 29, 2005

A redirect system is provided which is operable to redirect information over a network 1610. This information is associated with a compressed MP3 audio file which is initially transmitted through the network from a source 1612 to a user PC 1600. The user PC 1600 will then play the information and, upon playing the information, embedded information within the audio file will be detected by an...

System and apparatus for connecting a wireless device to a remote location on a network

United States 6,961,555

Issued November 1, 2005

A system for connecting a wireless device to a remote location on a computer network. The wireless device (2510) includes a processor (2714) and a transmitter/receiver (2716) for sending and receiving radio frequency signals (2516) to provide two-way digital communication between the processor and the computer network (306). The system comprises a beacon unit (2502) and a beacon signal receiver...

Launching a web site using a portable scanner

United States 6,877,032

Issued April 5, 2005

A method for a user to access information on a network. Information from a machine recognizable code (MRC) (1606) is extracted at a user location, which MRC (1606) has associated therewith routing information to a remote location (312) on the network. The extracted information from the MRC (1606) is wirelessly transmitted to a network interface device (302) in response to the information being...

Input device having positional and scanning capabilities

United States 6,868,433

Issued March 15, 2005

A multi-purpose input device (2500) for providing conventional positional tracking, and one or more read capabilities for automatically connecting a user PC (302) to remote node. In one embodiment, a user reads optically encoded indicia (1606) of a product by passing the input device (2500) thereover. A software interface (2505) processes the read information, assembles a message packet, and...

Optical reader and use

United States 6,860,424

Issued March 1, 2005

An optical reader is provided for reading a symbol representing information having areas of different light reflectivity. The optical reader comprises a radiant energy source, a photodetector, an optical system and a decoder. The radiant energy source generates a radiant energy for illuminating a target region. The photodetector generates output electrical signals indicative of the radiant energy...

Web site access manual of a character string into a software interface

United States 6,845,388

Issued January 18, 2005

An architecture for accessing a network server using one or more characters. A user computer (302) disposed on a global communication packet-switched network (306) is operable to communicate with an ARS (308) and a destination server (312) also disclosed on the GCN (306). The user computer (302) runs a software interface which displays a window (2500) to the user via a display (1612). The window...

Aiming indicia for a bar code and method of use

United States 6,843,417

Issued January 18, 2005

An aiming indicia is provided for a bar code comprising a sequence of parallel code bars and intervening code spaces disposed along a longitudinal code axis in accordance with a predefined standard. The aiming indicia comprises a non-encoded graphic element disposed on the longitudinal code axis adjacent the bar code and spaced apart from the nearest code bars by a distance of at least 10 times a...

Method and apparatus for tracking user profile and habits on a global network

United States 6,836,799

Issued December 28, 2004

A method and apparatus for tracking network activity of a user. A user PC (302) disposed on a network (306) runs tracking software which initially requires registration to a registration server (2500). The registration process is initiated by the user entering user information into the tracking software for transmission to the registration server (2500). In response to registration, the...

Method and apparatus for opening and launching a web browser in response to an audible signal

United States 6,829,650

Issued December 7, 2004

The present invention disclosed and claimed herein comprises a system and method for launching a web browser on a network comprising a computer having an all new input interface and a communication interface coupled to a computer network; said audio input coupled to the

audio output of a source for receiving an audio signal having encoded therein a unique code that is associated with a...

Presentation of web page content based upon computer video resolutions

United States 6,829,646

Issued December 7, 2004

An architecture for customizing the amount of web page banner advertising content presented to a user. When a user accesses a server node (102) disposed on a network (104), the user computer (100) provides video resolution information to the server node (102). The server node (102) transmits a web page to the user node (100) which corresponds to the video resolution information of the user node...

Digital ID for selecting web browser and use preferences of a user during use of a web application

United States 6,826,592

Issued November 30, 2004

A browser configuration architecture where input of a unique user ID automatically configures those browser applications preselected for auto-configuration from entries of a user preferences sheet. The user preferences sheet (2500) is part of the browser control software (2502) used for storing user preferences associated with one or more browser applications (2506, 2508, and 2510) loaded on a...

Method and apparatus for accessing a remote location with an optical reader having a programmable memory system

United States 6,823,388

Issued November 23, 2004

A method of accessing a remote location on a network using an optical reader. The optical reader includes an optical scanning system, a programmable memory system and an output circuit and is user-switchable between a scan mode, a record mode and a playback mode. The optical reader transmits a code to a first computer disposed on the network. When the optical reader is in the scan mode, the code...

Method for interfacing scanned product information with a source for the product over a global network

United States 6,816,894

Issued November 9, 2004

A method for interfacing scanned product information with a source for the product over a global network. A method is provided for obtaining information regarding the source of a product from a remote information source location on a global communication network utilizing a product code associated with the product and unique thereto. The product code associated with the product is scanned with a...

Method for configuring a piece of equipment with the use of an associated machine resolvable code

United States 6,792,452

Issued September 14, 2004

An architecture for automatically configuring equipment interfaced to a computer. A computer which is in communication with a network, is provided having the piece of equipment interfaced to the computer and having associated therewith one or more machine-resolvable codes (MRCs). The computer connects to a remote location disposed on the network in response to a select one of the one or more MRCs...

Method for conducting a contest using a network

United States 6,791,588

Issued September 14, 2004

A method for conducting a contest using a network is provided. A plurality of pick spaces, a virtual display fixture, and a plurality of virtual articles of commerce are displayed on the screen of a user computer. The user computer is disposed at a user site and operably connected to the network. Initially, the virtual articles of commerce are arrayed on the virtual display fixture. At least one...

Optical reader with ultraviolet wavelength capability

United States 6,758,398

Issued July 6, 2004

An optical reader is provided for reading a bar code having ultraviolet-wavelength-responsive properties. The optical reader includes an ultraviolet light source, a photodetector, an optical system and a decoder. The ultraviolet light source generates ultraviolet light having a wavelength shorter than visible light and longer than X-rays for illuminating a target region. The photodetector...

Bar code scanner and software interface interlock for performing encrypted handshaking and for disabling the scanner in case of handshaking operation failure

United States 6,757,715

Issued June 29, 2004

An interlocking architecture for a software interface and a bar code scanner. Upon power-up, a handshaking operation is performed between a scanner (1600) having a scanner processor (2600) and a computer processor (2612) of a computer (302) based upon the code stored in the NV memory (2602) of the scanner (1600) and a unique code associated with the software interface running on the computer...

Method and apparatus for accessing a remote location with an optical reader having a dedicated memory system

United States 6,754,698

Issued June 22, 2004

A method of accessing a remote location on a network using an optical reader. The optical reader has an optical scanning system and a dedicated address memory system. The optical scanning system, in response to the user scanning an encoded indicia therewith, sends to a first computer disposed on the network a scan code indicative of information encoded in the scanned indicia. The dedicated...

Method and apparatus for accessing a remote location by scanning an optical code

United States 6,745,234

Issued June 1, 2004

A method for controlling a computer is disclosed wherein one or more remote locations disposed on a network are accessed in response to scanning an optical code. A first computer disposed on the network connects to a scanner for scanning the optical code of a product by a user. The scanner is uniquely identified with a scanner distributor by a scanner identification number. A second computer...

Method and apparatus for configuring configurable equipment with configuration information received from a remote location

United States 6,725,260

Issued April 20, 2004

An architecture for automatically configuring equipment. A piece of equipment connected externally to a user PC has one or more machine-resolvable codes (MRCs) associated therewith. The piece of equipment receives configuration information from a remote location disposed on the network in response to reading a select one of the one or more MRCs with a reader. Configuration information associated...

Unique bar code for indicating a link between a product and a remote location on a web network

United States 6,708,208

Issued March 16, 2004

A unique bar code for indicating a link between a product and a remote location on a web network. The present invention dicsclosed and claimed herein, in one aspect thereof, comprises system for connecting between a first location at a user's site on a network and a second and remote location on a network. A unique ornamental symbol encoded with a plurality of dark and light areas is provided...

Automatic configuration of equipment software

United States 6,704,864

Issued March 9, 2004

An architecture for automatically configuring software of a piece of equipment. The piece of equipment is in communication with a network, the piece of equipment having one or more machine-resolvable codes associated therewith. The piece of equipment connects to a remote location disposed on the network in response to reading a select one of the one or more machine-resolvable codes with a reader....

Method and apparatus for accessing a remote location by sensing a machine-resolvable code

United States 6,701,369

Issued March 2, 2004

A method for controlling a computer wherein one or more remote locations disposed on a network are accessed in response to sensing a machine-resolvable code. A computer disposed on a network is operably connected to an input device for sensing a machine-resolvable code. A software application which includes a software identification code runs on the computer. In response to sensing a...

Method for interconnecting two locations over a network in response to using a tool

United States 6,701,354

Issued March 2, 2004

A method for accessing information over a network. A tool is utilized in conjunction with an operation on a user's processor at a user location on the network. The tool has associated therewith a unique tool ID. In response to utilizing the tool, the user's location is interconnected on the network to a predetermined destination at a remote location on the network, which destination has...

Method and apparatus for controlling a user's pc through an audio-visual broadcast to archive information in the users pc

United States 6,697,949

Issued February 24, 2004

A method for allowing a consumer to access an advertiser's location over a global communication network. A normal broadcast program is broadcast to a class of consumers having a unique signal embedded therein, which unique signal embedded therein is associated with a particular advertiser and a predetermined location on the network. Additionally, the unique signal has encoded therein a unique...

(PT) Método para conectar por meio de interface uma informação escaneada de produto a uma fonte do produto através de uma rede global

Mexico PI9913624

Issued January 15, 2002

(PT) "MéTODO PARA CONECTAR POR MEIO DE INTERFACE UMA INFORMAçãO ESCANEADA DE PRODUTO A UMA FONTE DO PRODUTO ATRAVéS DE UMA REDE GLOBAL". Método para conectar por meio de interface uma informação escaneada de produto com o fabricante do produto através de uma rede global de comunicação (306). Após escanear a informação de...

PI9913623 -Método para controlar um computador com um sinal de áudio

Europe PI9913623

Issued January 15, 2002

"MéTODO PARA CONTROLAR UM COMPUTADOR COM UM SINAL DE áUDIO". Método para controlar um computador (302) ao se inserir um sinal analógico (111) no computador (302)

para controlar um aplicativo de software navegador de rede. O sinal analógico (111) contém um sinal de acionamento que ativa um software de proprietário, e um identificador de produto. O...

Remote control having an optical indicia reader

United States 6,694,356

Issued February 17, 2004

A method for a user to access information on a network (306). A remote control device (3700) is provided operating in a first and control mode with internally generated control commands and in a second and scanning mode. In the control mode, an appliance at a user location is controlled by wirelessly transmitting the control commands to the appliance. In the scanning mode, a machine recognizable...

Unique bar code

United States 6,688,522

Issued February 10, 2004

A bar code for encoding information in machine-readable form is provided. The bar code comprises a character string including a plurality of characters disposed side-by-side along a longitudinal code axis. Each character is formed by a sequence of code bars and intervening code spaces, the code bars being parallel to one another and to a line defining a bar axis which intersects the code axis....

Method for controlling a computer using an embedded unique code in the content of video tape media

United States 6,643,692

Issued November 4, 2003

A method for allowing a user PC (1702) to be controlled in order to effect a connection between the user PC (1702) and a destination node (1706) on a network (306). This is facilitated through an audio source (1700) wherein the content of a video tape recording media has embedded therein an audio signal. When the video tape media is played, the audio signal is extracted by an audio extractor...

Method and apparatus for utilizing an audibly coded signal to conduct commerce over the internet

United States 6,636,896

Issued October 21, 2003

A method and apparatus for utilizing a coded audio/video signal to conduct commerce over the Internet. Broadcast information is broadcast from a remote location on a secondary network containing video over the secondary network to a location thereon proximate the location of the user PC. Unique information is encoded in the broadcast information representative of a location on the primary network...

Method for conducting a contest using a network

United States 6,636,892

Issued October 21, 2003

A method for conducting a contest using a network is provided. A plurality of pick spaces and a rolling counter are displayed on a screen of a computer operably connected to the network at a user site. The rolling counter constitutes successive ones of a plurality of available characters, each character being displayed for a preselected duration. Each time the user performs a predefined selection...

Method and system for conducting a contest using a network

United States 6,631,404

Issued October 7, 2003

A method for conducting a contest using a network. A selected article of commerce is identified to a plurality of users remotely disposed at user locations on the network which bears an indicia encoding an identification code which corresponds to the selected article in accordance with an extrinsic standard. An unvalidated entry message packet is then received at a reference location which was...

Interactive Doll

United States 6,629,133

Issued September 30, 2003

An interactive doll is disclosed having one or more sensors contained therein. The one or more sensors are operable to trigger output of a signal from the doll in response to the one or more sensors being activated by physical stimuli of a user. A processor located with the user and the doll at a first node of a global communication network processes the signal. The processor is operable to link...

Method and apparatus for allowing a remote site to interact with an intermediate database to facilitate access to the remote site

United States 6,622,165

Issued September 16, 2003

Method and apparatus for allowing a remote site to interact with an intermediate database to facilitate access to the remote site a method for delivering information from a source on a global communication network to a second and a user location thereon. A unique code is associated with an advertising action associated with the source location. The unique code is stored in a database and routing...

Method for controlling a computer using an embedded unique code in the content of dat media

United States 6,615,268

Issued September 2, 2003

A method for allowing a user PC to be controlled in order to effect a connection between the user PC and a destination node on a network. This is facilitated through an audio source wherein a digital audio tape recording media having embedded therein an audio signal therein.

When the recording media is played, the audio signal is extracted by an audio extractor and transmitted to the user PC, and...

Method and apparatus for utilizing an audibly coded signal to conduct commerce over the internet

United States 6,594,705

Issued July 15, 2003

A Method and apparatus for utilizing an audibly coded signal to conduct commerce over the Internet. Broadcast information is broadcast from a remote location on a secondary network over the secondary network to a location thereon proximate the location of the user PC on a primary network. Unique information is encoded in the broadcast information representative of a location on the primary...

Method and apparatus for controlling a computer from a remote location

United States 6,526,449

Issued February 25, 2003

A method for controlling a user computer is disclosed wherein a broadcast program is operable to transmit a broadcast to the user in the form of an audio/visual program, in addition to an encoded tone. This encoded tone is detected by the user computer and this information then transmitted to an intermediate node, an ARS (308). This tone is compared in a relational database (1704) to determine is...

Method and system for data transmission from an optical reader

United States 6,384,744

Issued May 7, 2002

A method is provided for transmitting data from an optical reader following scanning by the optical reader of an indica encoding information in accordance with one of a plurality of information encoding types. The method includes determining that a particular one of the plurality of encoding types was used for encoding the scanned indicia. A message packet is then transmitted from the optical...

Routing string indicative of a location of a database on a web associated with a product in commerce

United States 6,377,986

Issued April 23, 2002

A method for controlling a computer is disclosed wherein one or more remote locations disposed on a network are accessed in response to scanning an optical code. A first computer disposed on the network connects to a scanner for scanning the optical code of a product by a user. The scanner is uniquely identified with a scanner distributor by a scanner identification number. A second computer...

Keystroke Automator

United States D432,539

Issued October 24, 2000

The ornamental design for keystroke automator, as shown and described.

Method for controlling a computer with an audio signal

United States 6,098,106

Issued August 1, 2000

A method for controlling a computer by inputting an analog signal into the computer to control a web browser software application. The analog signal contains a trigger signal which activates proprietary software, and a product identifier. The proprietary software launches the web browser application on the computer, extracts the product identifier, and creates an appended data string by appending...

Method of product promotion

United States 6,928,413

Issued August 9, 2005

A method of promoting a product. A user at a user location (100) is induced to obtain a first product having a unique ID from a first vendor to win a prize. The user registers the product via a user computer (102) connected on-line to a central registration server (108) across a packet-switched network (104) by completing a user profile and transmitting the user profile and unique ID to a central...

Método para conectar por meio de interface uma informação escaneada de produto a uma fonte do produto através de uma rede global

Brazil PI9913624

Issued January 15, 2002

(PT) "MéTODO PARA CONECTAR POR MEIO DE INTERFACE UMA INFORMAçãO ESCANEADA DE PRODUTO A UMA FONTE DO PRODUTO ATRAVéS DE UMA REDE GLOBAL". Método para conectar por meio de interface uma informação escaneada de produto com o fabricante do produto através de uma rede global de comunicação (306). Após escanear a informação de...

Método para controlar um computador com um sinal de áudio

Brazil PI9913623

Issued January 15, 2002

"MéTODO PARA CONTROLAR UM COMPUTADOR COM UM SINAL DE áUDIO". Método para controlar um computador (302) ao se inserir um sinal analógico (111) no computador (302) para controlar um aplicativo de software navegador de rede. O sinal analógico (111) contém um sinal de acionamento que ativa um software de proprietário, e um identificador de produto. O...

INDICE DE POINTAGE DESTINE A UN CODE BARRES ET PROCEDE D'UTILISATION

France PCT/US2001/015970

Issued June 12, 2001

(FR)L'invention concerne un indice de pointage destiné à un code barres (4000), comportant une séquence de codes barres parallèles (4012) et d'espaces de code (4014) intercalés disposés le long d'un axe de code longitudinal (4010) selon un standard prédéfini. Ledit indice (4050) de pointage comporte un élément graphique (4052) non...

LECTEUR OPTIQUE ET UTILISATION CORRESPONDANTE

France WO/2001/093184

Issued December 6, 2001

L'invention concerne un lecteur optique permettant de lire un symbole qui représente une information dotée de zones de réflectivité de lumière différente. Le lecteur optique comporte une source d'énergie radiante, un photodétecteur, un système optique et un décodeur. Ladite source génère une énergie radiante permettant...

CODE BARRES UNIQUE

France WO/2001/093187

Issued December 6, 2001

L'invention concerne un code barres destiné à coder des informations sous forme lisible par machine. Ce code barres comporte une chaîne de caractères contenant une pluralité de caractères disposés l'un à côté de l'autre le long d'un axe de code longitudinal. Chaque caractère est formé par une séquence de codes barres...

Input device for allowing interface to a web site in association with a unique input code

United States 8,069,098

Issued November 29, 2011

An input device for allowing interface to a web site in association with a unique input code. A method for interconnecting a first location on a global communication network with a second location thereon is disclosed. An input device is provided at the first location on the global communication network having associated therewith a unique input device ID. A product code disposed on a product is...

(FR) INDICE DE POINTAGE DESTINE A UN CODE BARRES ET PROCEDE D'UTILISATION

Europe WO/2001/093190

Issued

(FR)L'invention concerne un indice de pointage destiné à un code barres (4000), comportant une séquence de codes barres parallèles (4012) et d'espaces de code (4014) intercalés disposés le long d'un axe de code longitudinal (4010) selon un standard prédéfini. Ledit indice (4050) de pointage comporte un élément graphique (4052) non...

(FR) INDICE DE POINTAGE DESTINE A UN CODE BARRES ET PROCEDE D'UTILISATION

Europe WO/2001/093190

Issued June 12, 2001

FR)L'invention concerne un indice de pointage destiné à un code barres (4000), comportant une séquence de codes barres parallèles (4012) et d'espaces de code (4014) intercalés disposés le

long d'un axe de code longitudinal (4010) selon un standard prédéfini. Ledit indice (4050) de pointage comporte un élément graphique (4052) non...

Method and apparatus for accessing a remote location by sensing a machine-resolvable code

United States 8,484,362

Issued July 9, 2013

A method for controlling a computer wherein one or more remote locations disposed on a network are accessed in response to sensing a machine-resolvable code. A computer disposed on a network is operably connected to an input device for sensing a machine-resolvable code. A software application which includes a software identification code runs on the computer. In response to sensing a...

2 inventors:

-
  Hutton (Jovan) Pulitzer
  Founder FevrTech.org, Flip.Ventures, Xplrr.org and Publisher at InvestigatingHistory.org

- **J Jovan Philyaw**

Method and apparatus for accessing a remote location with an optical reader having a programmable memory system

United States 8,296,440

Issued October 23, 2012

An optical reader for accessing a remote location on a network includes an optical scanning system, a memory system, an output circuit for interfacing to a first computer disposed on the network, and a switching device for switching between a scan mode, a record mode and a playback mode. The optical reader further includes a transmitter for transmitting code information representative of a code...

3 inventors:

-
  Hutton (Jovan) Pulitzer
  Founder FevrTech.org, Flip.Ventures, Xplrr.org and Publisher at InvestigatingHistory.org

- **j hutton pulitzer**
-
  Doug Davis
  EVP Technology at West Corporation

Input device for allowing interface to a web site in association with a unique input code

United States 8,069,098

Issued November 29, 2011

An input device for allowing interface to a web site in association with a unique input code. A method for interconnecting a first location on a global communication network with a second location thereon is disclosed. An input device is provided at the first location on the global communication network having associated therewith a unique input device ID. A product code disposed on a product is...

2 inventors:

- **Hutton (Jovan) Pulitzer**
  Founder FevrTech.org, Flip.Ventures, Xplrr.org and Publisher at InvestigatingHistory.org

- **J Jovan Philyaw**

Method and apparatus for accessing a remote location by sensing a machine-resolvable code

United States 8,484,362

Issued July 9, 2013

A method for controlling a computer wherein one or more remote locations disposed on a network are accessed in response to sensing a machine-resolvable code. A computer disposed on a network is operably connected to an input device for sensing a machine-resolvable code. A software application which includes a software identification code runs on the computer. In response to sensing a...

Method and apparatus for accessing a remote location with an optical reader having a programmable memory system

United States 8,296,440

Issued September 23, 2012

An optical reader for accessing a remote location on a network includes an optical scanning system, a memory system, an output circuit for interfacing to a first computer disposed on the network, and a switching device for switching between a scan mode, a record mode and a playback mode. The optical reader further includes a transmitter for transmitting code information representative of a code...

(EN) AUTOMATIC CONFIGURATION OF EQUIPMENT AND SOFTWARE (FR) CONFIGURATION AUTOMATIQUE D'EQUIPEMENT ET DE LOGICIEL

Europe WO/2001/086435

Issued October 5, 2001

(EN)An architecture for automatically configuring equipment. A piece of equipment connected externally to a user PC has one or more machine-resolvable codes (MRCs) associated therewith.

The piece of equipment receives configuration information from a remote location disposed on the network in response to reading a select one of the one or more MRCs with a reader. Configuration information...

Method and apparatus for accessing a remote location by sensing a machine-resolvable code

United States 8,484,362

Issued July 9, 2013

A method for controlling a computer wherein one or more remote locations disposed on a network are accessed in response to sensing a machine-resolvable code. A computer disposed on a network is operably connected to an input device for sensing a machine-resolvable code. A software application which includes a software identification code runs on the computer. In response to sensing a...

 2 inventors:

- **Hutton (Jovan) Pulitzer**
  Founder FevrTech.org, Flip.Ventures, Xplrr.org and Publisher at InvestigatingHistory.org

- **jeffry jovan philyaw**

Method for controlling a computer using an embedded unique code in the content of recorded media

United States 8,655,972

Issued February 18, 2014

A method for controlling a computer with recorded information of a recorded media includes embedding a unique code, which unique code does not contain routing information, in recorded information of the recorded media. The unique code is in close association with vendor information, such that the unique code will be output during normal playback of the information on the recorded media. The...

 2 inventors:

- **Hutton (Jovan) Pulitzer**
  Founder FevrTech.org, Flip.Ventures, Xplrr.org and Publisher at InvestigatingHistory.org

- **jeffry jovan philyaw**

Method and apparatus for linking a web browser link to a promotional offer

United States 8,712,835

Issued April 29, 2014

A method for offering a promotion to a user. A stimulus is received from a broadcast directed to a user location, the stimulus having unique coded information encoded therein. The unique coded information is extracted from the stimulus by decoding this information. From the decoded information, there is determined routing information for routing over a network to a promotion location on the...

2 inventors:

Hutton (Jovan) Pulitzer
Founder FevrTech.org, Flip.Ventures, Xplrr.org and Publisher at InvestigatingHistory.org

- **jeffry jovan philyaw**

Method and apparatus for accessing a remote location with an optical reader having a programmable memory system

United States 8,296,440
Issued October 23, 2012

An optical reader for accessing a remote location on a network includes an optical scanning system, a memory system, an output circuit for interfacing to a first computer disposed on the network, and a switching device for switching between a scan mode, a record mode and a playback mode. The optical reader further includes a transmitter for transmitting code information representative of a code...

2 inventors:

Hutton (Jovan) Pulitzer
Founder FevrTech.org, Flip.Ventures, Xplrr.org and Publisher at InvestigatingHistory.org

- **Jeffry Jovan Philyaw**

Method and apparatus for accessing a remote location by sensing a machine-resolvable code

United States 8,484,362
Issued July 9, 2013

A method for controlling a computer wherein one or more remote locations disposed on a network are accessed in response to sensing a machine-resolvable code. A computer disposed on a network is operably connected to an input device for sensing a machine-resolvable code. A software application which includes a software identification code runs on the computer. In response to sensing a...

US00D432539S

United States Patent [19]

Philyaw

[11] **Patent Number:** **Des. 432,539**

[45] **Date of Patent:** ✱✱ **Oct. 24, 2000**

[54] **KEYSTROKE AUTOMATOR**

[75] Inventor: **Jeffry Jovan Philyaw**, Dallas, Tex.

[73] Assignee: **DigitalConvergence.:Com Inc.**, Dallas, Tex.

[**] Term: **14 Years**

[21] Appl. No.: **29/116,705**

[22] Filed: **Jan. 7, 2000**

[51] **LOC (7) Cl.** **14-02**
[52] **U.S. Cl.** **D14/426**; D14/420
[58] **Field of Search** D14/420, 426,
D14/427, 432, 402, 403, 405, 407, 409,
417; 235/472.01, 472.02, 472.03, 375; 345/156–167;
200/5 R, 5 A, 6 R, 6 A; 273/148 B; 74/471 XY;
463/36, 37, 38

[56] **References Cited**

U.S. PATENT DOCUMENTS

D. 343,829	2/1994	Okuda et al.	D14/426
D. 352,939	11/1994	Karlin	D14/426
D. 375,748	11/1996	Hartman	D14/417
D. 381,661	7/1997	Althans	D14/417
D. 385,263	10/1997	Taylor	D14/407

Primary Examiner—Kay H. Chin
Attorney, Agent, or Firm—Howison, Chauza, Handley & Arnott, LLP

[57] **CLAIM**

The ornamental design for keystroke automator, as shown and described.

DESCRIPTION

FIG. **1** is top view of a keystroke automator showing my new design;
FIG. **2** is right side view of the keystroke automator;
FIG. **3** is bottom view of the keystroke automator;
FIG. **4** is a left side view of the keystroke automator;
FIG. **5** is a front view of the keystroke automator; and,
FIG. **6** is rear view of the keystroke automator.
The broken lines shown in FIGS. **1** through **6** drawing are for illustrative purposes only and form no part of the claimed design.

1 Claim, 2 Drawing Sheets

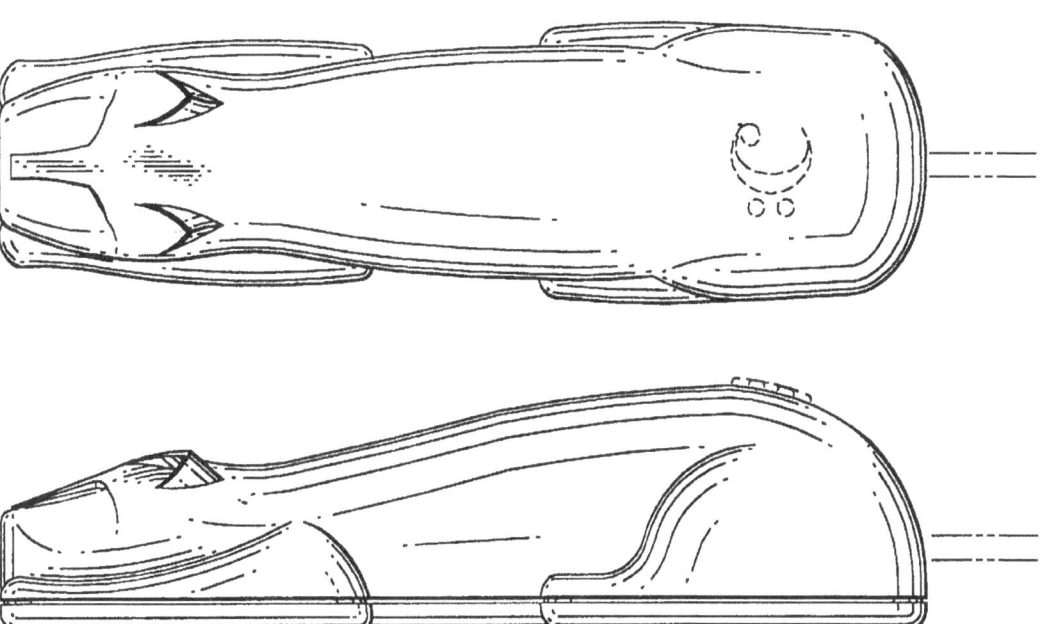

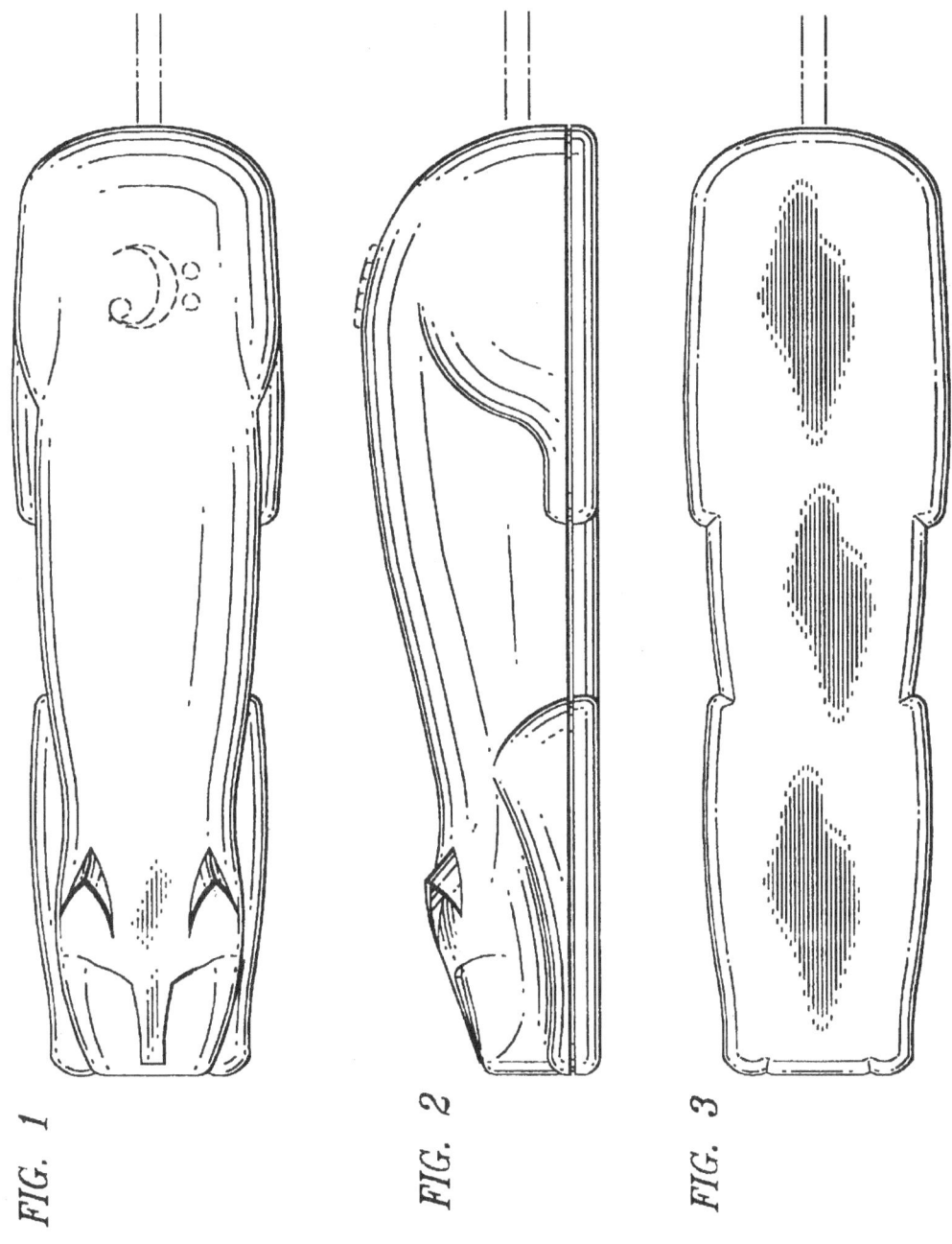

FIG. 1

FIG. 2

FIG. 3

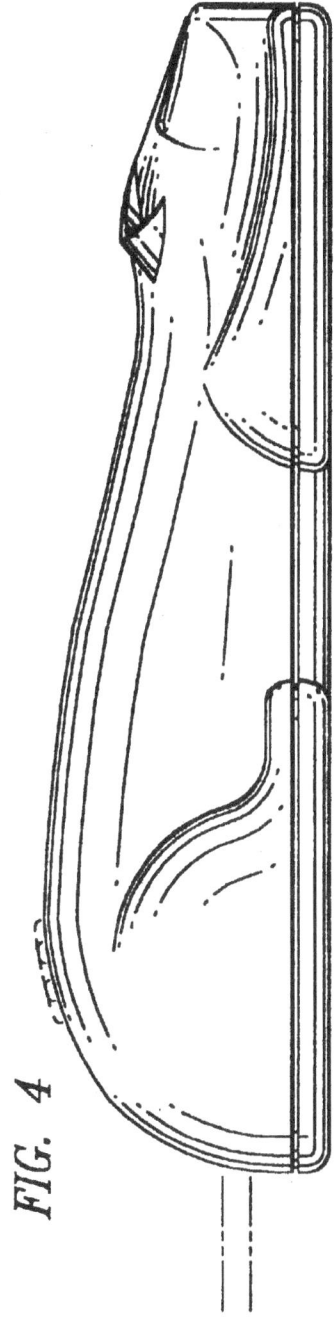

FIG. 4

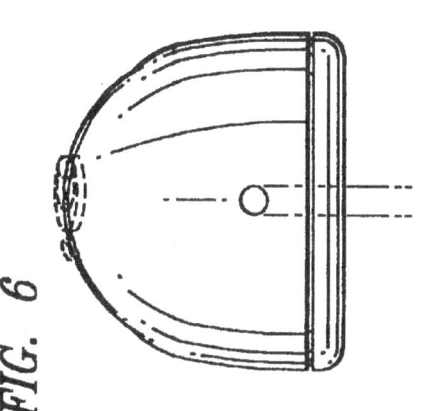

FIG. 6

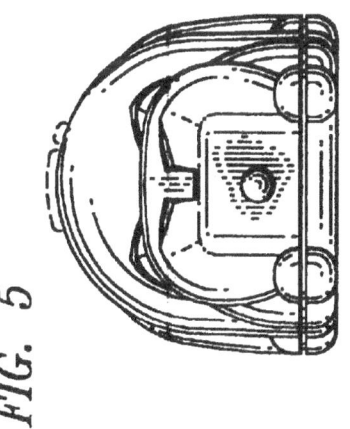

FIG. 5

United States Patent [19]

Philyaw

[11] Patent Number: **Des. 432,539**

[45] Date of Patent: ** **Oct. 24, 2000**

US00D432539S

[54] **KEYSTROKE AUTOMATOR**

[75] Inventor: **Jeffry Jovan Philyaw**, Dallas, Tex.

[73] Assignee: **DigitalConvergence.:Com Inc.**, Dallas, Tex.

[**] Term: **14 Years**

[21] Appl. No.: **29/116,705**

[22] Filed: **Jan. 7, 2000**

[51] **LOC (7) Cl.** **14-02**

[52] **U.S. Cl.** **D14/426**; D14/420

[58] **Field of Search** D14/420, 426,
D14/427, 432, 402, 403, 405, 407, 409,
417; 235/472.01, 472.02, 472.03, 375; 345/156–167;
200/5 R, 5 A, 6 R, 6 A; 273/148 B; 74/471 XY;
463/36, 37, 38

[56] **References Cited**

U.S. PATENT DOCUMENTS

D. 343,829	2/1994	Okuda et al.	D14/426
D. 352,939	11/1994	Karlin	D14/426
D. 375,748	11/1996	Hartman	D14/417
D. 381,661	7/1997	Althans	D14/417
D. 385,263	10/1997	Taylor	D14/407

Primary Examiner—Kay H. Chin
Attorney, Agent, or Firm—Howison, Chauza, Handley & Arnott, LLP

[57] **CLAIM**

The ornamental design for keystroke automator, as shown and described.

DESCRIPTION

FIG. **1** is top view of a keystroke automator showing my new design;

FIG. **2** is right side view of the keystroke automator;

FIG. **3** is bottom view of the keystroke automator;

FIG. **4** is a left side view of the keystroke automator;

FIG. **5** is a front view of the keystroke automator; and,

FIG. **6** is rear view of the keystroke automator.

The broken lines shown in FIGS. **1** through **6** drawing are for illustrative purposes only and form no part of the claimed design.

1 Claim, 2 Drawing Sheets

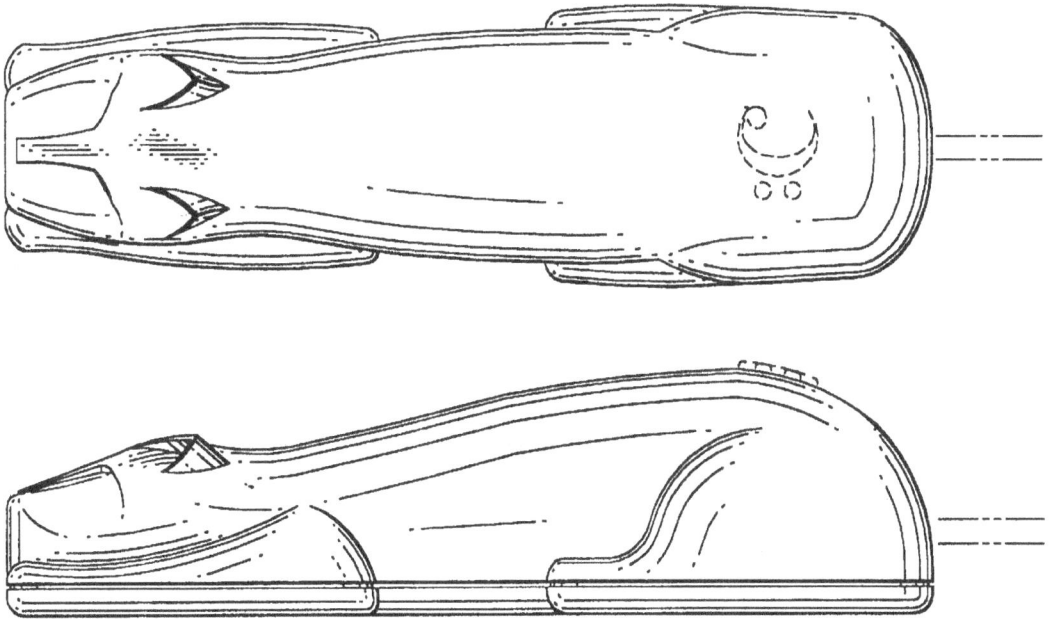

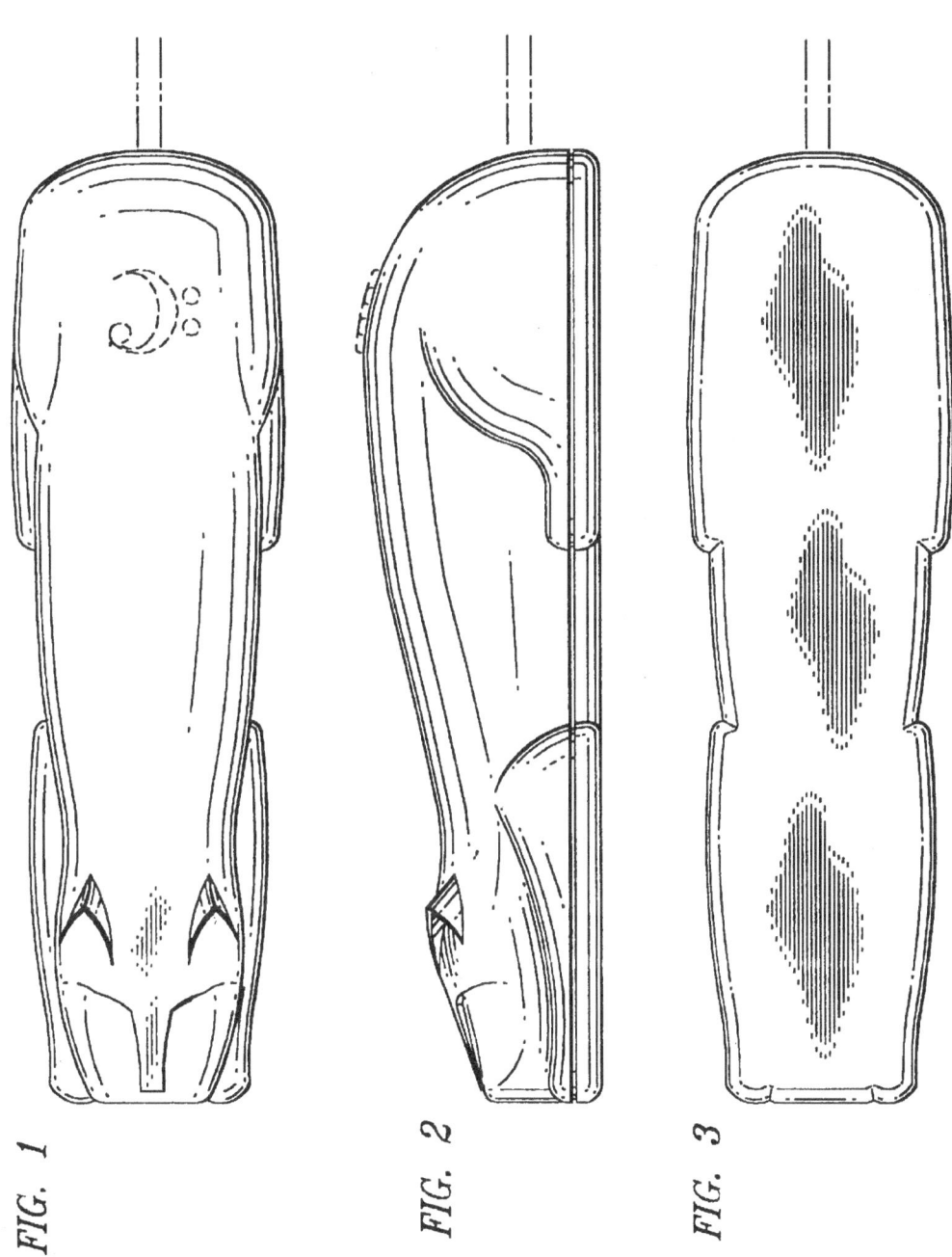

FIG. 1

FIG. 2

FIG. 3

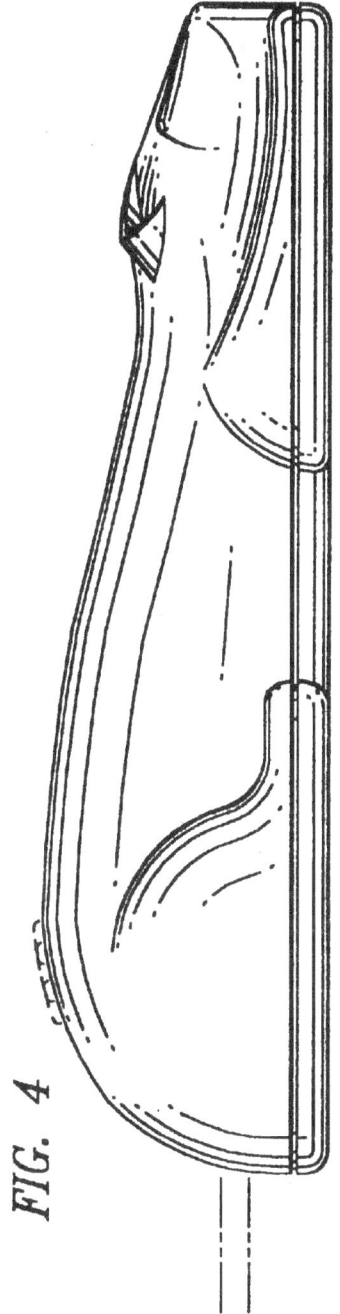

FIG. 4

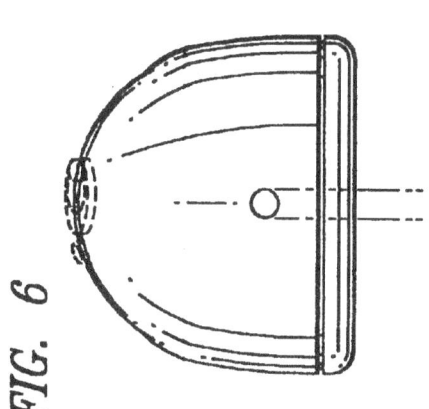

FIG. 6

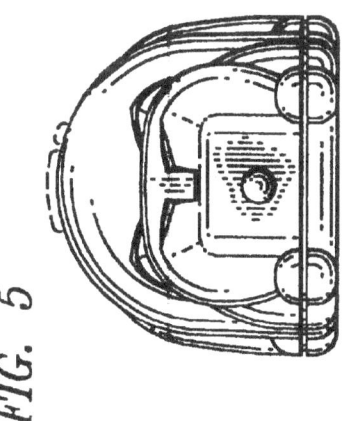

FIG. 5

United States Patent [19]

Philyaw

[11] **Patent Number:** **Des. 432,539**

[45] **Date of Patent:** ** **Oct. 24, 2000**

[54] **KEYSTROKE AUTOMATOR**

[75] Inventor: **Jeffry Jovan Philyaw**, Dallas, Tex.

[73] Assignee: **DigitalConvergence.:Com Inc.**, Dallas, Tex.

[**] Term: **14 Years**

[21] Appl. No.: **29/116,705**

[22] Filed: **Jan. 7, 2000**

[51] **LOC (7) Cl.** **14-02**
[52] **U.S. Cl.** **D14/426**; D14/420
[58] **Field of Search** D14/420, 426,
D14/427, 432, 402, 403, 405, 407, 409,
417; 235/472.01, 472.02, 472.03, 375; 345/156–167;
200/5 R, 5 A, 6 R, 6 A; 273/148 B; 74/471 XY;
463/36, 37, 38

[56] **References Cited**

U.S. PATENT DOCUMENTS

D. 343,829	2/1994	Okuda et al.	D14/426
D. 352,939	11/1994	Karlin	D14/426
D. 375,748	11/1996	Hartman	D14/417
D. 381,661	7/1997	Althans	D14/417
D. 385,263	10/1997	Taylor	D14/407

Primary Examiner—Kay H. Chin
Attorney, Agent, or Firm—Howison, Chauza, Handley & Arnott, LLP

[57] CLAIM

The ornamental design for keystroke automator, as shown and described.

DESCRIPTION

FIG. **1** is top view of a keystroke automator showing my new design;
FIG. **2** is right side view of the keystroke automator;
FIG. **3** is bottom view of the keystroke automator;
FIG. **4** is a left side view of the keystroke automator;
FIG. **5** is a front view of the keystroke automator; and,
FIG. **6** is rear view of the keystroke automator.
The broken lines shown in FIGS. **1** through **6** drawing are for illustrative purposes only and form no part of the claimed design.

1 Claim, 2 Drawing Sheets

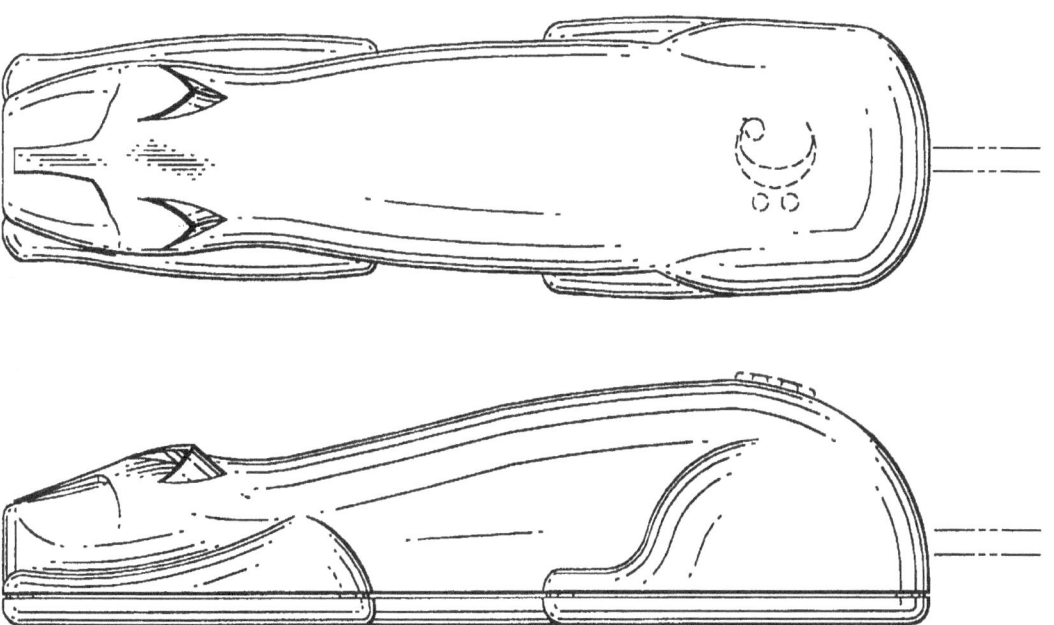

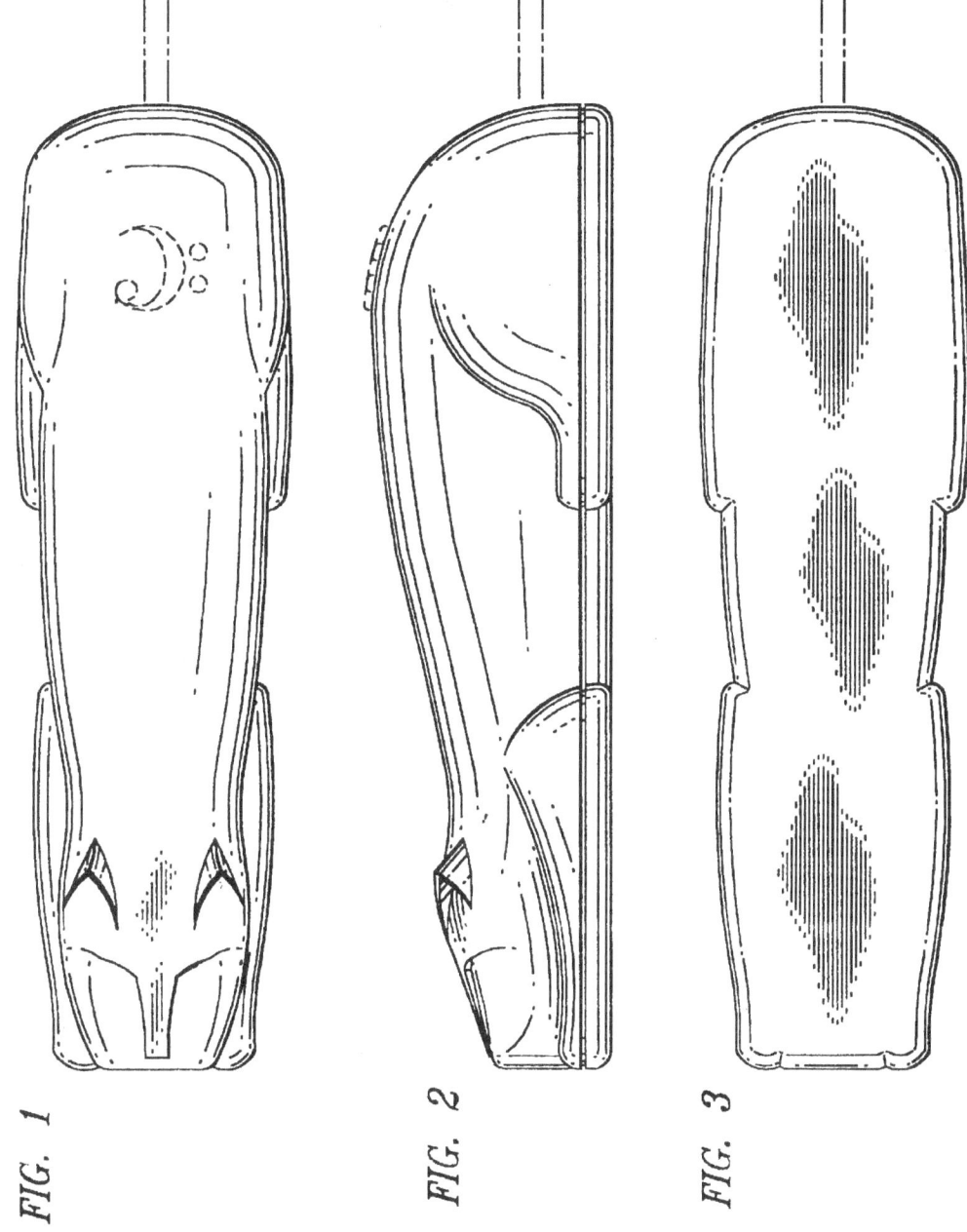

FIG. 1

FIG. 2

FIG. 3

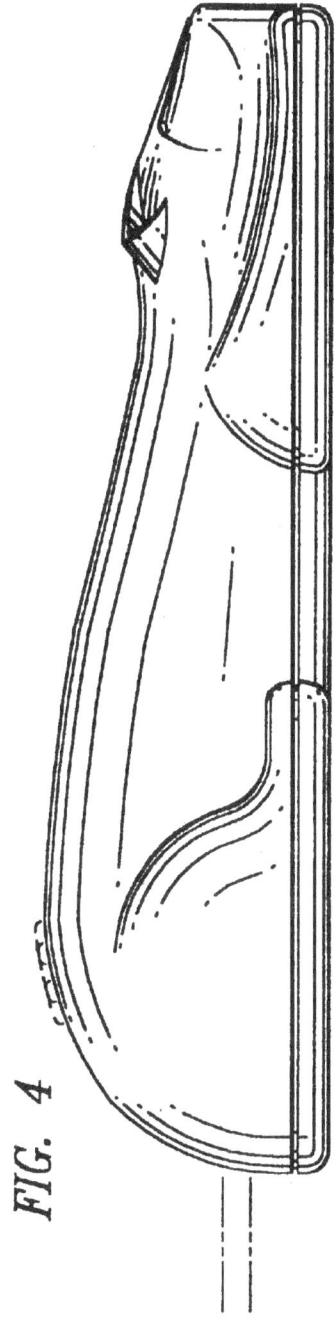

FIG. 4

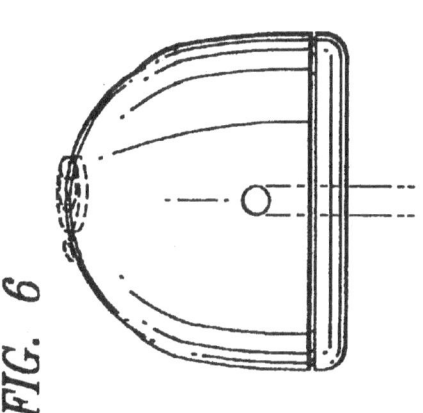

FIG. 6

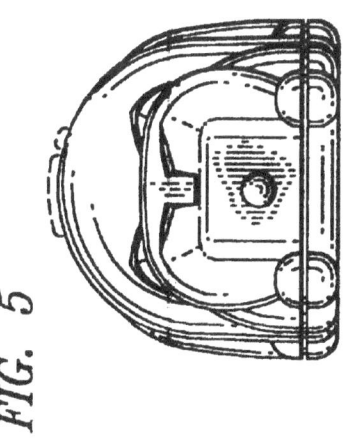

FIG. 5

US00D432539S

United States Patent [19]

Philyaw

[11] **Patent Number:** **Des. 432,539**

[45] **Date of Patent:** ✷✷ **Oct. 24, 2000**

[54] **KEYSTROKE AUTOMATOR**

[75] Inventor: **Jeffry Jovan Philyaw**, Dallas, Tex.

[73] Assignee: **DigitalConvergence.:Com Inc.**, Dallas, Tex.

[**] Term: **14 Years**

[21] Appl. No.: **29/116,705**

[22] Filed: **Jan. 7, 2000**

[51] **LOC (7) Cl.** **14-02**

[52] **U.S. Cl.** **D14/426**; D14/420

[58] **Field of Search** D14/420, 426,
D14/427, 432, 402, 403, 405, 407, 409,
417; 235/472.01, 472.02, 472.03, 375; 345/156–167;
200/5 R, 5 A, 6 R, 6 A; 273/148 B; 74/471 XY;
463/36, 37, 38

[56] **References Cited**

U.S. PATENT DOCUMENTS

D. 343,829	2/1994	Okuda et al.	D14/426
D. 352,939	11/1994	Karlin	D14/426
D. 375,748	11/1996	Hartman	D14/417
D. 381,661	7/1997	Althans	D14/417
D. 385,263	10/1997	Taylor	D14/407

Primary Examiner—Kay H. Chin
Attorney, Agent, or Firm—Howison, Chauza, Handley & Arnott, LLP

[57] **CLAIM**

The ornamental design for keystroke automator, as shown and described.

DESCRIPTION

FIG. **1** is top view of a keystroke automator showing my new design;

FIG. **2** is right side view of the keystroke automator;

FIG. **3** is bottom view of the keystroke automator;

FIG. **4** is a left side view of the keystroke automator;

FIG. **5** is a front view of the keystroke automator; and,

FIG. **6** is rear view of the keystroke automator.

The broken lines shown in FIGS. **1** through **6** drawing are for illustrative purposes only and form no part of the claimed design.

1 Claim, 2 Drawing Sheets

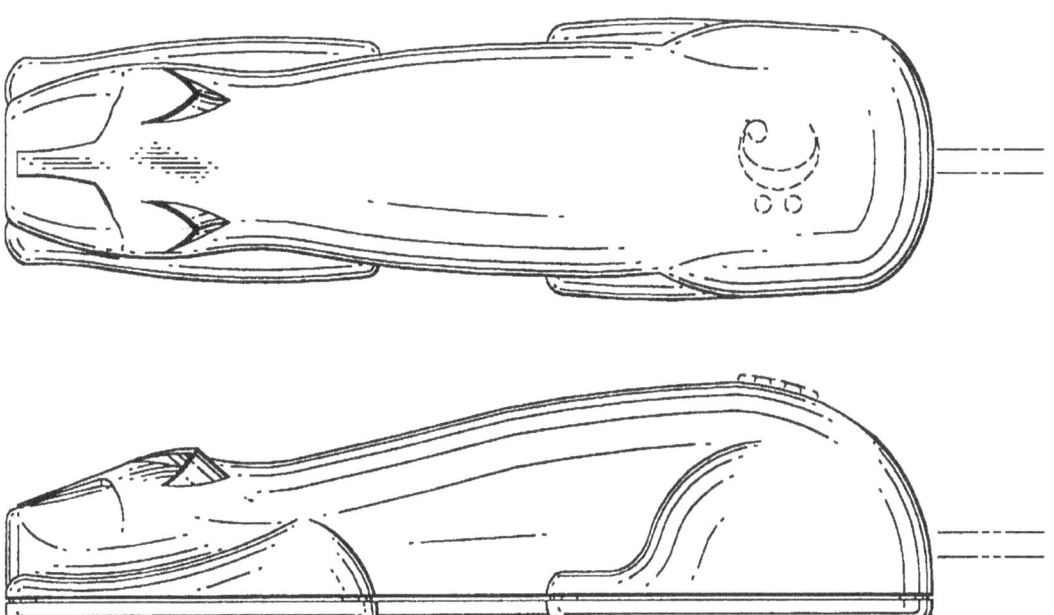

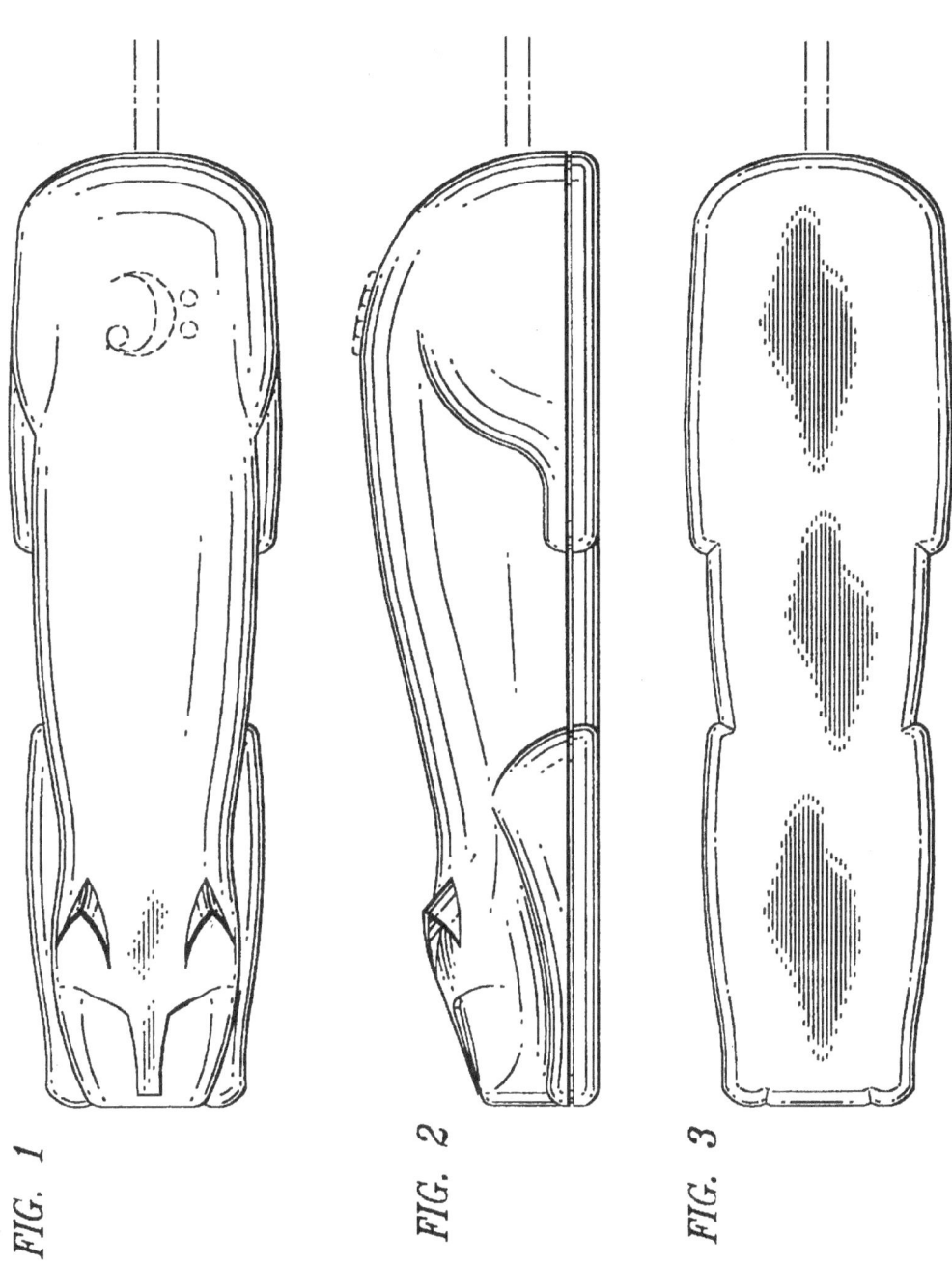

FIG. 1

FIG. 2

FIG. 3

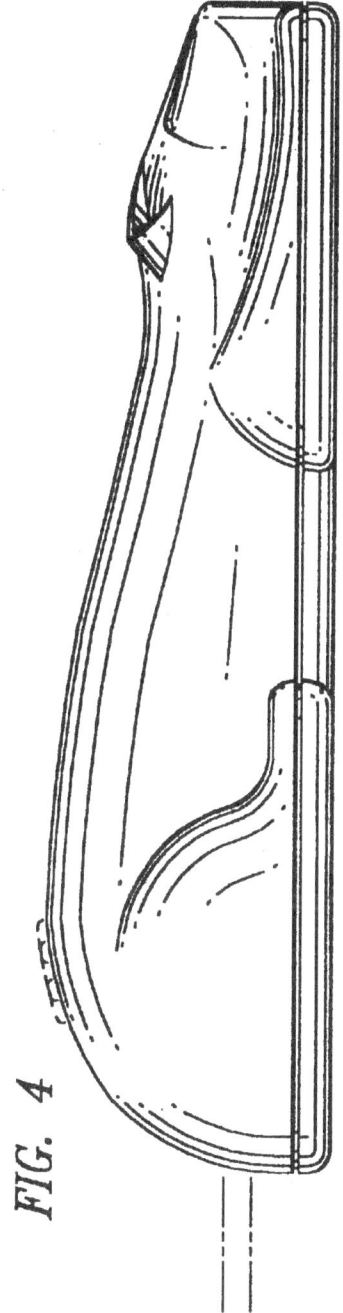

FIG. 4

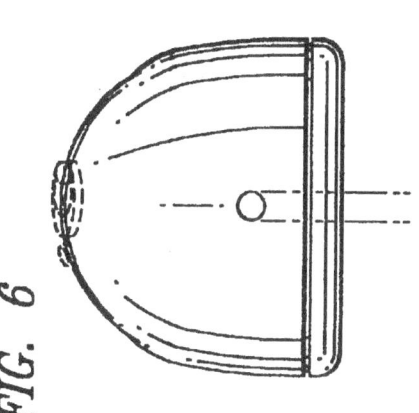

FIG. 6

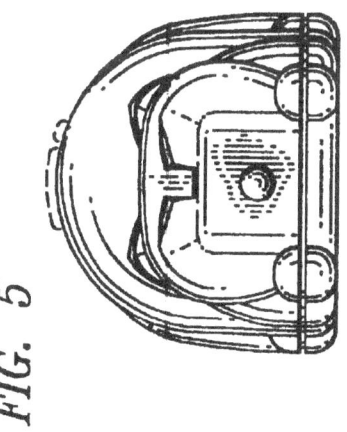

FIG. 5

US00D432539S

United States Patent [19]

Philyaw

[11] **Patent Number:** **Des. 432,539**

[45] **Date of Patent:** ** **Oct. 24, 2000**

[54] **KEYSTROKE AUTOMATOR**

[75] Inventor: **Jeffry Jovan Philyaw**, Dallas, Tex.

[73] Assignee: **DigitalConvergence.:Com Inc.**, Dallas, Tex.

[**] Term: **14 Years**

[21] Appl. No.: **29/116,705**

[22] Filed: **Jan. 7, 2000**

[51] **LOC (7) Cl.** **14-02**
[52] **U.S. Cl.** **D14/426**; D14/420
[58] **Field of Search** D14/420, 426,
D14/427, 432, 402, 403, 405, 407, 409,
417; 235/472.01, 472.02, 472.03, 375; 345/156–167;
200/5 R, 5 A, 6 R, 6 A; 273/148 B; 74/471 XY;
463/36, 37, 38

[56] **References Cited**

U.S. PATENT DOCUMENTS

D. 343,829	2/1994	Okuda et al.	D14/426
D. 352,939	11/1994	Karlin	D14/426
D. 375,748	11/1996	Hartman	D14/417
D. 381,661	7/1997	Althans	D14/417
D. 385,263	10/1997	Taylor	D14/407

Primary Examiner—Kay H. Chin
Attorney, Agent, or Firm—Howison, Chauza, Handley & Arnott, LLP

[57] **CLAIM**

The ornamental design for keystroke automator, as shown and described.

DESCRIPTION

FIG. **1** is top view of a keystroke automator showing my new design;
FIG. **2** is right side view of the keystroke automator;
FIG. **3** is bottom view of the keystroke automator;
FIG. **4** is a left side view of the keystroke automator;
FIG. **5** is a front view of the keystroke automator; and,
FIG. **6** is rear view of the keystroke automator.
The broken lines shown in FIGS. **1** through **6** drawing are for illustrative purposes only and form no part of the claimed design.

1 Claim, 2 Drawing Sheets

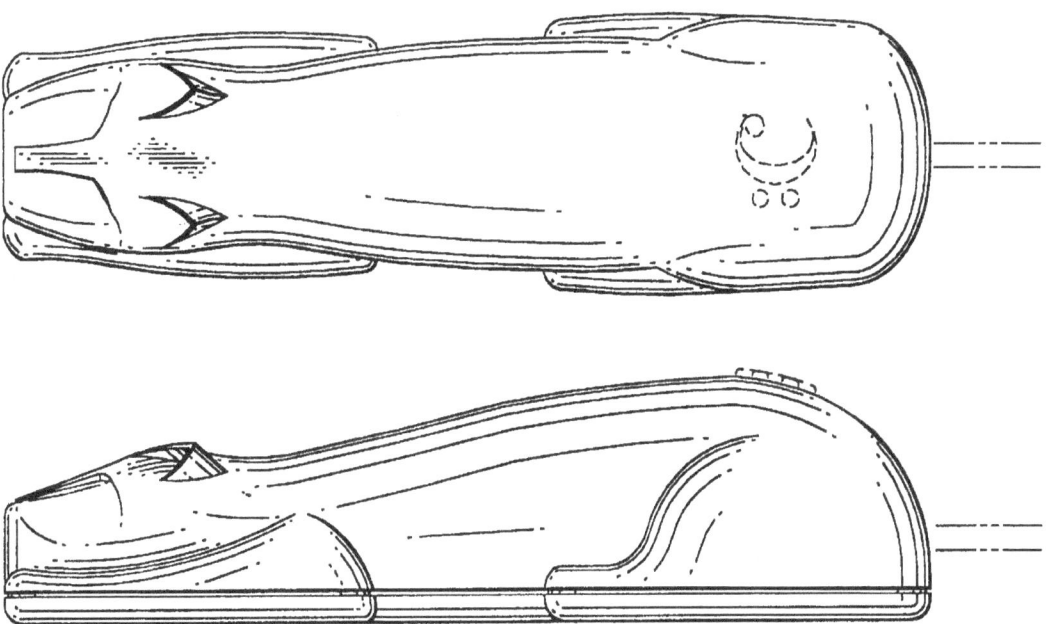

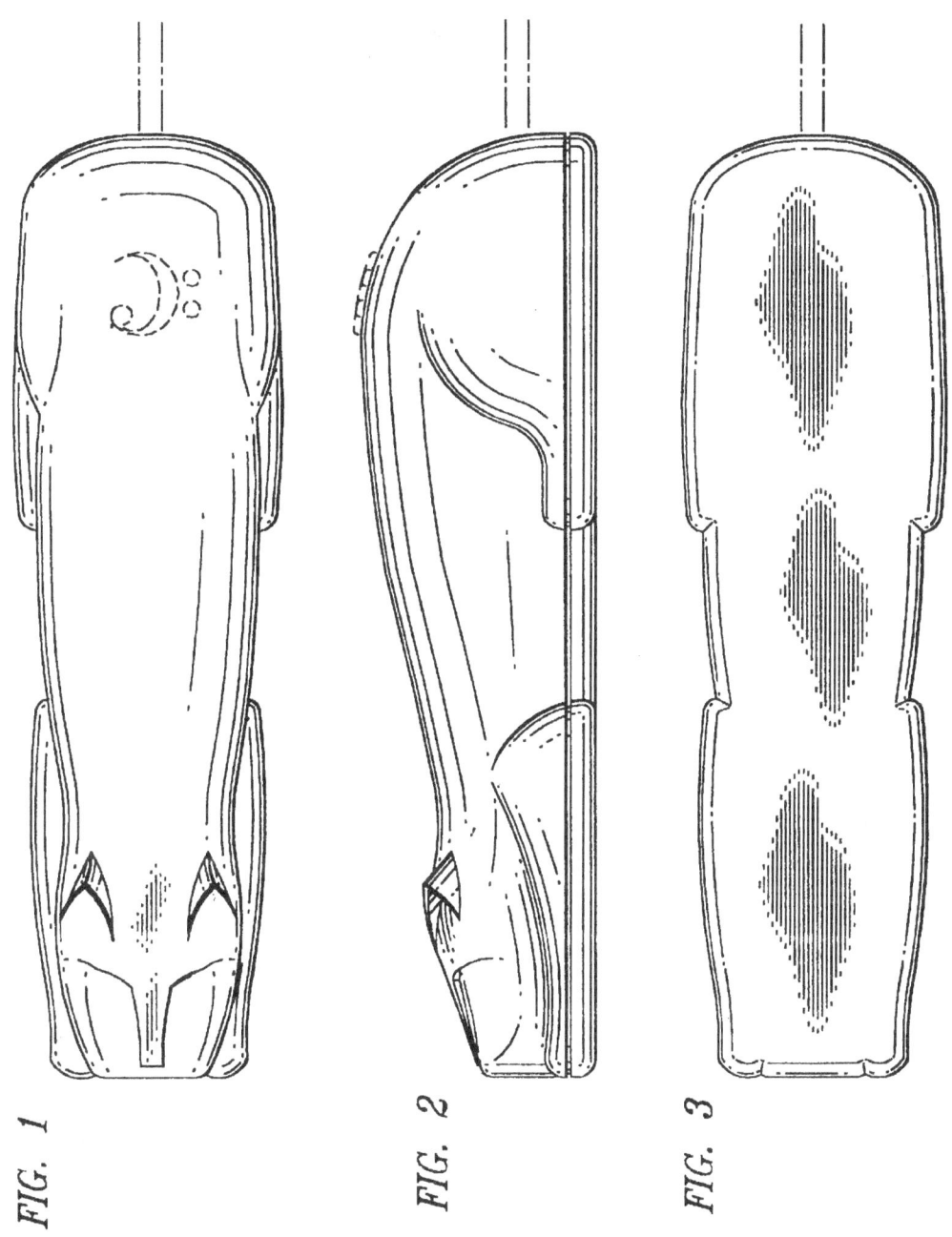

FIG. 1

FIG. 2

FIG. 3

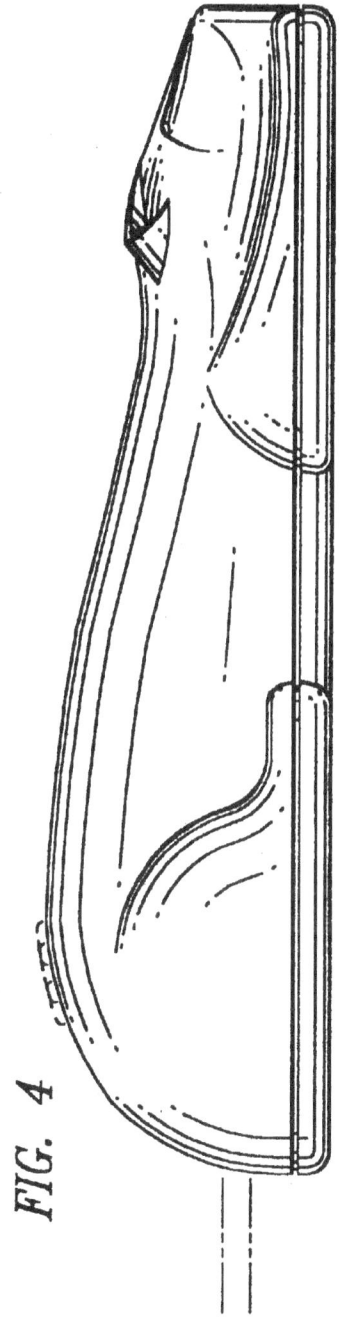

FIG. 4

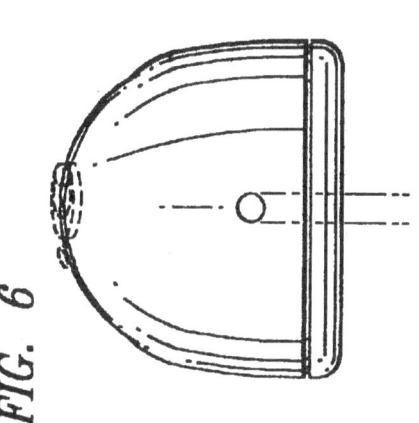

FIG. 6

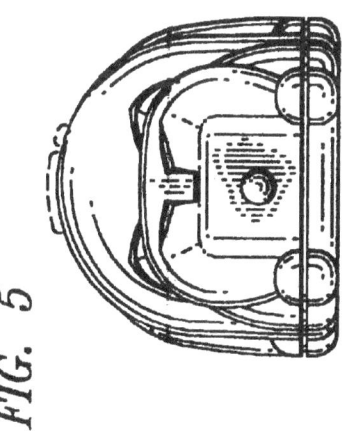

FIG. 5

United States Patent [19]

Philyaw

US00D432539S

[11] Patent Number: Des. 432,539

[45] Date of Patent: ** Oct. 24, 2000

[54] **KEYSTROKE AUTOMATOR**

[75] Inventor: **Jeffry Jovan Philyaw**, Dallas, Tex.

[73] Assignee: **DigitalConvergence.:Com Inc.**, Dallas, Tex.

[**] Term: **14 Years**

[21] Appl. No.: **29/116,705**

[22] Filed: **Jan. 7, 2000**

[51] **LOC (7) Cl.** **14-02**

[52] **U.S. Cl.** **D14/426**; D14/420

[58] **Field of Search** .... D14/420, 426, D14/427, 432, 402, 403, 405, 407, 409, 417; 235/472.01, 472.02, 472.03, 375; 345/156–167; 200/5 R, 5 A, 6 R, 6 A; 273/148 B; 74/471 XY; 463/36, 37, 38

[56] **References Cited**

U.S. PATENT DOCUMENTS

D. 343,829	2/1994	Okuda et al.	D14/426
D. 352,939	11/1994	Karlin	D14/426
D. 375,748	11/1996	Hartman	D14/417
D. 381,661	7/1997	Althans	D14/417
D. 385,263	10/1997	Taylor	D14/407

Primary Examiner—Kay H. Chin
Attorney, Agent, or Firm—Howison, Chauza, Handley & Arnott, LLP

[57] **CLAIM**

The ornamental design for keystroke automator, as shown and described.

DESCRIPTION

FIG. 1 is top view of a keystroke automator showing my new design;
FIG. 2 is right side view of the keystroke automator;
FIG. 3 is bottom view of the keystroke automator;
FIG. 4 is a left side view of the keystroke automator;
FIG. 5 is a front view of the keystroke automator; and,
FIG. 6 is rear view of the keystroke automator.
The broken lines shown in FIGS. 1 through 6 drawing are for illustrative purposes only and form no part of the claimed design.

1 Claim, 2 Drawing Sheets

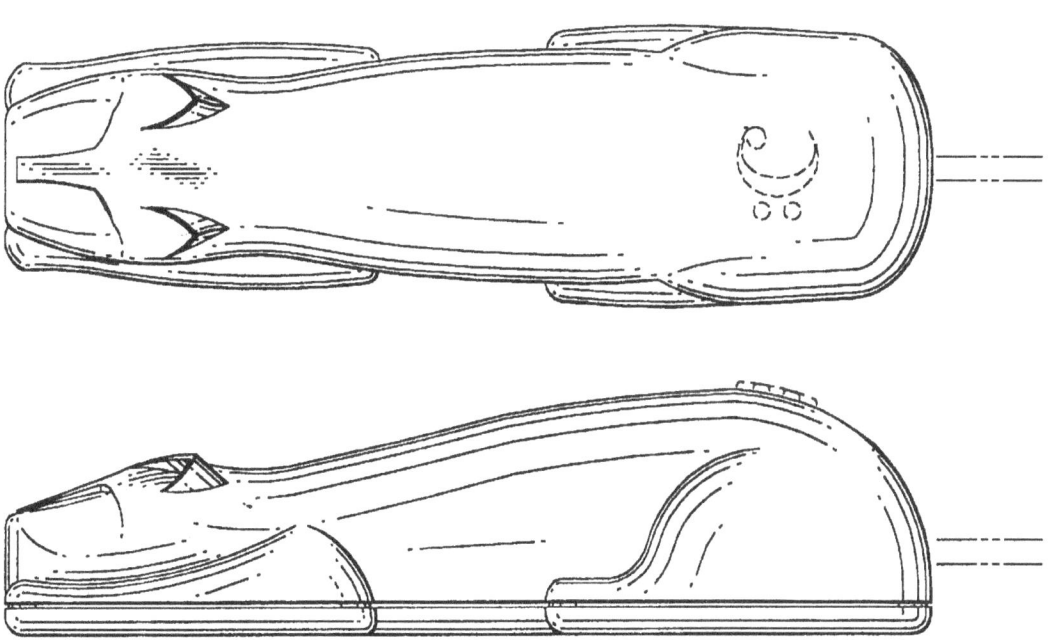

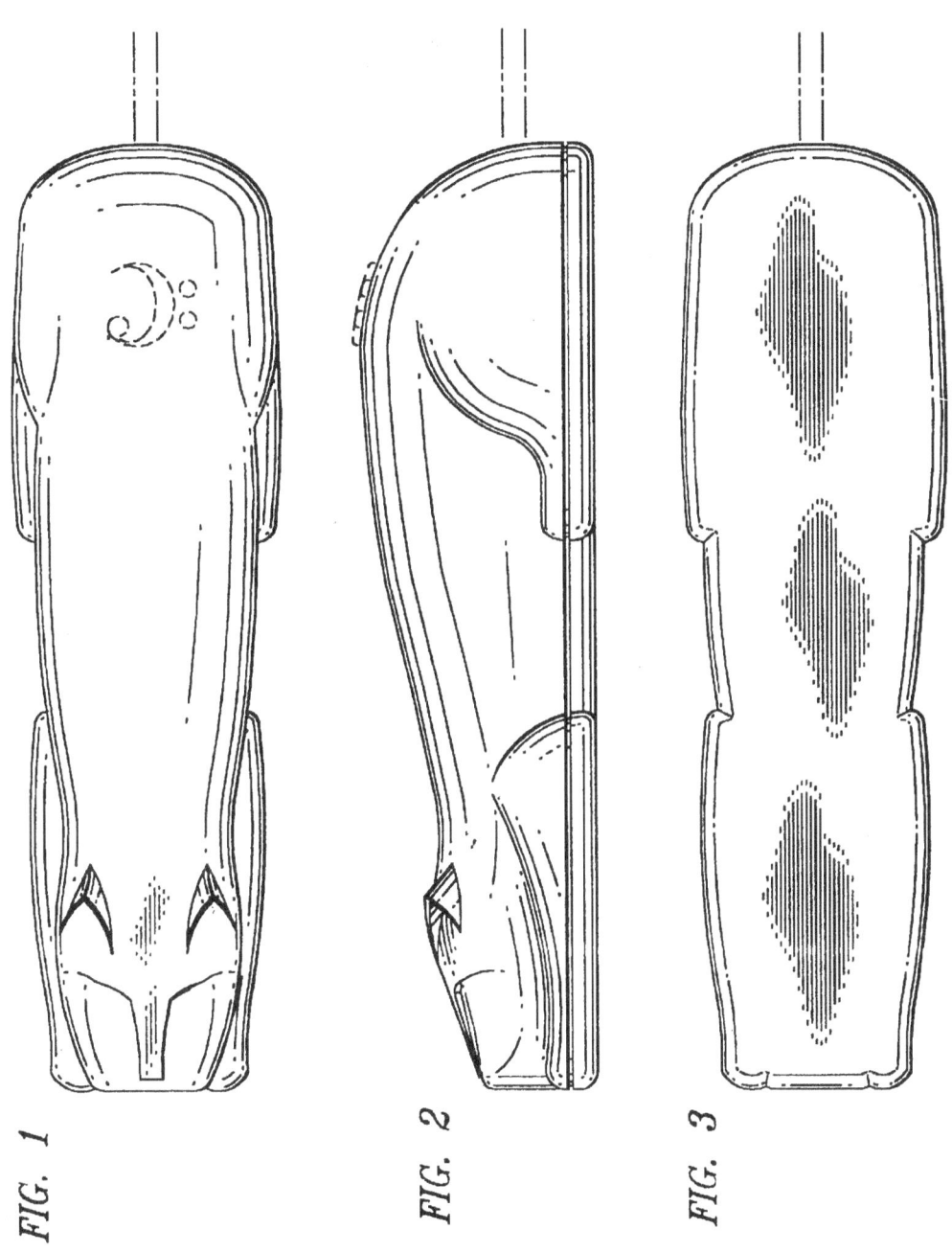

FIG. 1

FIG. 2

FIG. 3

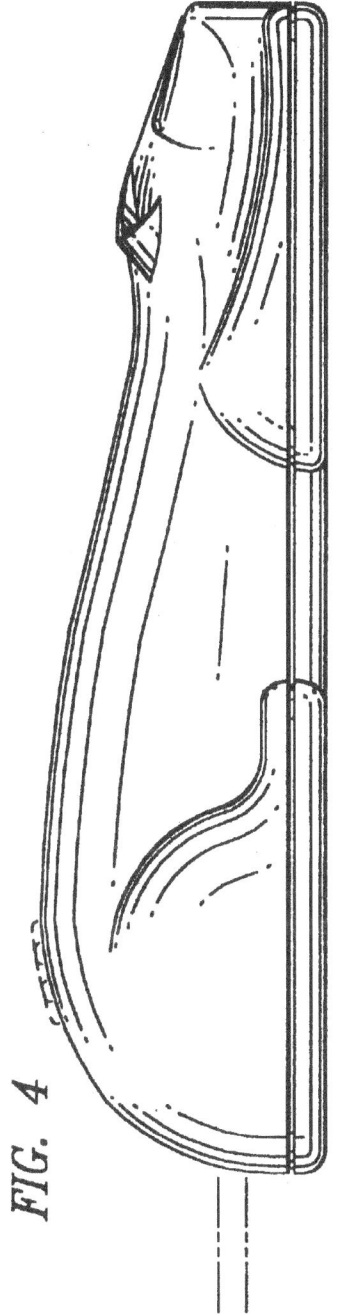

FIG. 4

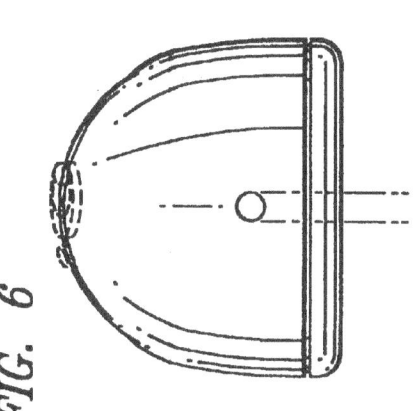

FIG. 6

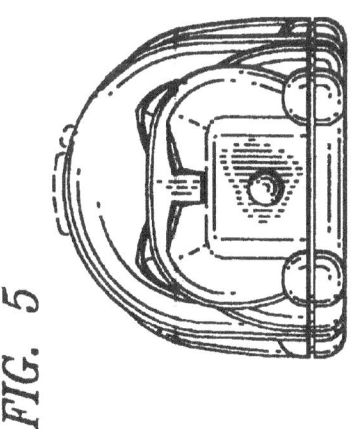

FIG. 5

www.ingramcontent.com/pod-product-compliance
Lightning Source LLC
Chambersburg PA
CBHW081835280526
45789CB00007B/2462